ST. MARY'S UNIVERSITY COLLEGE
LIBRARY
A COLLEGE OF THE QUEENS UNIVERSITY OF BELFAST

Tel. 028 90327678
Web site www.stmarys-belfast.ac.uk
email: library@stmarys-belfast.ac.uk

Fines will be charged for overdue and recalled books not returned by
stated date.

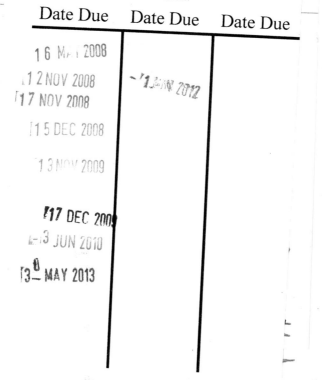

Introduction

This is not a book that I had ever anticipated writing. When my colleagues and I first introduced our program in "Contemporary Moral Issues" at the Massachusetts Institute of Technology, I was opposed to our including the question of abortion as part of the curriculum. It seemed to me that in fact there was no real issue of the kind—that the moral opposition to abortion one still encountered was based solely upon dubious theological claims. However, when abortion did become one of the topics treated in the course, I rapidly realized that I was wrong. Indeed, as I studied the subject it became clear to me, to my considerable surprise, that there was reason to doubt that abortion was ever morally justifiable. This book is an account of the considerations that led me to this new conclusion.

It is, I am aware, not a popular conclusion, and I must make clear, as I undertake to explain it, that I comprehend and have due regard for the arguments that have led others to quite different conclusions, though to say that is obviously not to say that I think that they are right. I am particularly sensitive, too, to what are deeply felt convictions on the part of some women that access to abortion is a basic condition of their own liberation. As I have invested a considerable ideation in the development of my point of view, a portion of them have as well. What is more, a portion have displayed an extraordinary energy in advancing their views, particularly in the legislative area, as they have sought to overturn old statutes preventing abortion and, now, to prevent a legislative reversal of the change that they have been instrumental in bringing about. Many women have been keenly aware, simply because of their own sexual identities, what the social and personal penalties are of a lack of access to abortion. It has even been suggested to male philosophers that they cannot express authentic judgments on the question of abortion because their sex disqualifies them from doing so. That is an assertion that I cannot accept, and I cannot accept it because I have seen no convincing evidence that our own humanity, male and female alike, is not a far more powerful integrative principle of understanding than such differences in the characteristics of that humanity. Besides, in the arguments that women have made, I have not seen any evidence of an intellectual or emotional awareness that seems alien to me.

I regret the nature of some of the support, however inadvertently, a position like mine is bound to attract. But that consideration cannot still my argument. I would like to point out, however, that if all the moral tenderness that rises in some quarters so self-righteously against abortion had been turned in decades past to an alleviation of those conditions that have driven so many individuals to seek abortions, I think we should find the crucial judgment we now must make much easier. Any individual or group that now *only* opposes abortion seems to me immediately suspect.

Four observations. It is hard to talk about abortion without speaking philosophy, but the nature of that discourse may be of some surprise to those not used to it. It is replete with examples, often extraordinary, designed to clarify an argument by setting it in a situation so extreme or unexpected as to refresh our view of the argument or to lead to an irresistible conclusion. Indeed, the literature is filled with talking cats or chimps, movie stars with healing hands, Frankensteins, and other creatures of the kind. That is the way we seem to have to argue, and, as will be observed, I am not immune from this inclination.

The second observation is that the language of philosophy can be so abstract that the lay reader may fall into the mistake of assuming that philosophers are having arguments for argument's sake. If ever that observation is correct, it is not so with reference to an issue as pressing as the one under discussion here—an issue that has, moreover, delicate ramifications in many other areas. The abstractness of the language of philosophy is due, instead, to the philosopher's desire to discuss such a pressing issue in a reasoned manner, without appeal to mere emotions.

The third observation is that I do not recall a single paper that cannot be said to argue from basic moral assumptions or intuitions (the exposition of these, it will be noticed, is often preceded by the word "surely"). I do not disguise my own assumptions, but I should like it to be noted that in making them I am not indulging in some

Abortion and the Sanctity of Human Life

The MIT Press
Cambridge, Massachusetts, and London, England

Abortion and the Sanctity of Human Life:
A Philosophical View

Baruch Brody

Copyright © 1975 by
The Massachusetts Institute of Technology

This book was set in IBM Composer Press Roman
by Jay's Publishers Services, Inc.
printed on Finch Title 93,
and bound
by The Colonial Press Inc.
in the United States of America

Library of Congress Cataloging in Publication Data

Brody, Baruch A
    Abortion and the sanctity of human life.

    1. Abortion–United States. I. Title. [DNLM: 1. Abortion, Induced.
HQ767 B864a]
HQ767.5.U5B76   301   75–4662
ISBN 0–262–02–116–1

To My Students in Contemporary Moral Issues

Contents

rite of mystery. I appeal rather often to the reader's moral intuitions because it seems to me that our moral intuitions are a significant part of the data against which our moral theories are tested. To say this, however, is not to say that our moral intuitions are always correct; indeed, there are occasions on which I will explicitly argue for retaining a particular theory at the cost of rejecting some of our moral intuitions. All that I am presupposing is that any moral theory that is in conflict with our moral intuitions should be rejected unless overwhelming reasons can be given for disregarding those intuitions.

The final point is terminological. When, in this book, I use the phrase "human being," I mean "a member of the species Homo sapiens who has a right to life similar to the right to life had by you, me, and so on." My initial assumption that the fetus is a human being is an assumption about its rights, and not merely about the species to which it belongs. Although this terminological point is implicit throughout the book, I want to make it explicitly clear at the outset so as to avoid any possible misunderstanding.

My book is divided into three parts. In Part I, I start with the assumption that the fetus becomes a human being at some point before birth and argue from that assumption that abortion is morally justifiable only in certain very rare circumstances and that there should be laws prohibiting abortions. In Part II, I examine my initial assumption. I discover it to be correct, and in particular I conclude that the fetus becomes a human being during the second month after conception.

Although this sequence may seem strange, I adopted it for the following reason: many adherents of the so-called permissive or liberal position about abortion maintain that abortions are morally permissible, or, at least, that there should be no laws prohibiting abortions even if the fetus is a human being. The attractiveness of this claim is clear; it enables its adherents to hold their permissive position without having to defend the questionable claim that the fetus does not become a human being until its birth (or, perhaps, until some time after that). It therefore seems to me essential to remove this possibility, to argue that the permissive position can only be based upon some claim about the status of the fetus. This is what I try to do in Part I. Having done so, I turn, in Part II, to a consideration of that status.

In Part III, I consider several less central but still extremely important issues. These include the rights of the fetus before it becomes a human being and the responsibilities of society to pregnant women, particularly those whose pregnancy is burdensome or physically or psychologically dangerous. I also discuss the Supreme Court's recent decisions on the constitutionality of abortion laws. Rather than dealing on a piecemeal basis with aspects of that decision throughout the book, I postpone consideration of it until Chapter 9. In that chapter, the decision is subjected to a careful analysis in light of the theoretical discussion in the main part of the book.

About half of this book contains material drawn (with heavy modifications) from articles of mine that appeared in R. Perkin's *Abortion* and in the following journals: *American Philosophical Quarterly*, *Journal of Philosophy*, *Nous*, *Philosophia*, and *Philosophy and Public Affairs*. I want to thank Professor Perkins and the relevant editors for permission to reprint that material. I would also like to thank Frances Kamm and Jerry Dworkin for having been very patient in listening to some of the ideas I have had and for responding to them, Professor Paul Ramsey for making some helpful suggestions about an earlier draft of this book, and Howard Webber, whose sympathetic help was immensely valuable. Finally, in dedicating this book to the students in my course, I am only partially repaying them for their many ideas and arguments that I have appropriated here. The rabbis must have had such students in mind when they said: "I have learnt much from my teachers, and even more from my colleagues. But I have learnt the most from my students."

Part I

1 The Morality of Abortion (1)

Perhaps our most fundamental moral intuition is that it is wrong to take the life of another human being. Nearly as fundamental, however, is the intuition that under certain circumstances it is permissible to do so. Such exceptions have historically been very difficult of definition—that observation is apparent from the most casual inspection of the exceptions condoned in the past. There are obvious conflicts among them, and one suspects that at least some of these exceptions have been allowed out of political or other special interests.

The clearest exception is self-defense. If the life of one human being is threatened by the actions of another, then the first human being may, all else failing, defend himself, even to the point of taking the life of the second. I should like to explore, in this chapter, the following issue: let us suppose that there is some point (and now it is not necessary to try to establish that point) in the development of the fetus when that fetus is properly regarded as a human being; and let us imagine, further, a case in which the woman carrying the fetus discovers, at some time after that point, that she herself will die unless she aborts the fetus. Is it permissible for her to abort the fetus in order to save her own life? Is this one of the extreme circumstances in which it is permissible to take the life of another human being? Is this, in short, legitimate self-defense?

1.1 Abortion and Self-defense

Why would not it be permissible for the mother to have an abortion in order to save her life even after that point at which the fetus becomes a human being? After all, the fetus's continued existence poses a threat to the life of the mother, and why can't she void that threat by taking the life of the fetus, as an ultimate act of defense?

To be sure, it may be the physician, or other agent, who will cause the abortion, and not the mother herself, but that difference seems to be irrelevant. Our intuition is that the person whose life is threatened (call that person A) may either take the life of the person (B) who threatens his life or call upon someone else (*C*) to do so. And more important, it seems permissible (and perhaps even obligatory in some cases) for *C* to take *B's* life in order to save *A*'s life.[1] Put in traditional terms, we are really speaking of the mother's right as the pursued, or anyone else's right as an onlooker, to take the life of the fetus who is the pursuer.

Pope Pius XI observed,[2] in objecting to this argument from self-defense, that in the paradigm case of killing the pursuer *B* is unjustly attempting to take *A*'s life and is responsible for that attempt. It is the resulting guilt, based in part on *B*'s intention (found in the attempt to kill *A*), together with the fact that *A* will die unless *B* is stopped, which permits the taking of *B*'s life. The reader will notice that the abortion situation is quite different. Leaving aside for now—we shall return to it later on—the question as to whether the fetus can properly be described as attempting to take the mother's life, we can certainly agree that the fetus is not responsible for such an attempt (if it is occurring), that the fetus is therefore innocent, not guilty, and that the taking of fetal life cannot be compared to the paradigm case of killing the pursuer.

There is another way of putting Pope Pius's point. Consider the following case: there is, let us imagine, a medicine that *A* needs to stay alive, *C* owns some, and *C* will give it to *A* only if *A* kills *B*. Moreover, *A* has no other way of getting the medicine. In this case, the continued existence of *B* certainly poses a threat to the life of *A; A* can survive only if *B* does not survive. Still, it is not permissible for *A* to kill *B* in order to save *A*'s life. Why not? How does this case differ from the paradigm case of killing the pursuer? The simplest answer is that in this case, while *B*'s continued existence poses a threat to the life of *A, B* is not guilty of attempting to take *A*'s life because there is no attempt to be guilty about in the first place. Now if we consider the case of a fetus whose continued existence poses a threat to the life of the mother, we see that it is like the medicine case and not like the paradigm case of killing the pursuer. The fetus does pose (in our imagined situation) a threat to the life of its mother, but it is not guilty of attempting to take its mother's life. Consequently, in an analogue to the medicine case, the mother (or her agent) could not justify destroying the fetus on the ground that it would be a permissible act of killing the pursuer.

The persuasiveness of both of the preceding arguments indicates that we have to analyze the whole issue of pursuit far more carefully before we can definitely decide whether an abortion to save the life of the mother could be viewed as a permissible act of killing the pursuer. If we look again at a paradigm case of pursuit, we see that there are three factors involved:

1. The continued existence of B poses a threat to the life of A, a threat that can be met only by the taking of B's life (we shall refer to this as the condition of danger).

2. B is unjustly attempting to take A's life (we shall refer to this as the condition of attempt).

3. B is responsible for his attempt to take A's life (we shall refer to this as the condition of guilt).

In the medicine case, only the danger condition was satisfied. Our intuitions that it would be wrong for A to take B's life in that case reflects our belief that the mere fact that B is a danger to A is not sufficient to establish that killing B will be a justifiable act of killing a pursuer. But it would be rash to conclude, as Pope Pius did, that all three conditions must be satisfied before the killing of B will be a justifiable act of killing a pursuer. What would happen, for example, if the first two conditions, but not the guilt condition, were satisfied?

There are good reasons for supposing that the satisfaction of the first two conditions is sufficient justification for taking B's life as an act of killing the pursuer. Consider, for example, a variation of the pursuit paradigm—one in which B is about to shoot A, and the only way by which A can stop him is by killing him first—but one in which B is a minor who is not responsible for his attempt to take A's life.[3] In this case, the only condition not satisfied is the condition of guilt. Still, despite that fact, is seems that A may justifiably take B's life as a permissible act of killing a pursuer. The guilt of the pursuer, then, is not a requirement for legitimacy in killing the pursuer.

Are there any cases in which the satisfaction of the danger condition and something weaker than the attempt condition is sufficient to justify A's killing B as an act of killing a pursuer? It seems that there may be. Consider, for example, the following case: B is about to press a button that turns on a light, and there is no reason for him to suspect what is the case, that is, that his doing so will also explode a bomb that will destroy A. Moreover, the only way in which we can stop B and save A's life is by taking B's life, for there is no opportunity to warn B of the actual consequences of his act. In such a case, B is not attempting to take A's life and, a fortiori, he is neither responsible for nor guilty of any such attempt. Nevertheless, this may still be a case in which there is justification for taking B's life in order to save A's life; that is, this may still be a legitimate case of killing a pursuer.

It is important to keep in mind that although we may kill B to save A, it does not follow—and indeed it is not true—that A should be punished if he does blow up B. As we shall see later, there is an important difference in this respect between punishment and preventive killing.

How does this case differ from the medicine case? Or, to put our question another way, what condition, in addition to the danger condition, is satisfied in this case but not in the medicine case, so that its satisfaction (together with the satisfaction of the danger condition) is sufficient to justify our killing B as an act of killing a pursuer? As we think about the two cases, the following idea suggests itself: there is, in this most recent example, some action that B is doing (pressing the button) that will result in A's death, an action that if taken in full knowledge and voluntarily would result in B's[4] being responsible for the loss of A's life. Even if performed without full knowledge and intent, this action itself justifies the taking of B's life. In the medicine case, on the other hand, no such action is performed. C may well be to blame for the loss of A's life if he does not give A the medicine when A refuses to kill B. But this has nothing to do with B. It would seem then that A is justified in taking B's life as an act of killing a pursuer if, in addition to B's being a danger to A, the following condition is satisfied:

2. B is doing some action that will lead to A's death, and that action is such that if B were a responsible person who did it voluntarily knowing that this result would come about, B would be responsible for the loss of A's life (we shall refer to this as the condition of action).

To summarize, then, our general discussion of killing the pursuer, we can say the following: the mere satisfaction of the danger condition is not sufficient to justify the killing of the pursuer. If, in addition, either the attempt condition or the condition of action is satisfied, then one would be justified in killing the pursuer to save the life of the pursued. In any case, the condition of guilt, arising from full knowledge and intent, need not be satisfied.

These results wreak havoc with a very plausible analysis of why it is permissible to take the life of the pursuer to save the life of the pursued. It seemed at one point that it was the guilt of the pursuer that justified the taking of his life to save that of the pursued. This presupposes that the pursuer performs his attempt knowledgeably and intentionally. We have just seen that this is not so; the mere action is sufficient justification.[5] So the analysis in question must be rejected.

Let us return now to the problem of abortion and apply these results to the case of the fetus whose continued existence poses a threat to the life of his mother. Is it permissible, as an act of killing a pursuer, to abort the fetus in order to save the mother? The first thing that we should note is that Pope Pius's objection to aborting the fetus as a permissible act of killing a pursuer is mistaken. His objection is that the fetus shows no knowledge or intention in his attempt to take the life of the mother, that the fetus is, in a word, innocent. But that only means that the condition of guilt is not satisfied, and we have seen that its satisfaction is not necessary.

Is, then, the aborting of the fetus, when necessary to save the life of the mother, a permissible act of killing a pursuer? It is true that in such cases the fetus is a danger to the mother. But it is also clear that the condition of attempt is not satisfied. The fetus has neither the beliefs nor the intentions to which we have referred. Furthermore, there is on the part of the fetus no action that threatens the life of the mother. So not even the condition of action is satisfied.[6] It seems to follow, therefore, that aborting the fetus could not be a permissible act of killing a pursuer.

It is instructive, in this light, to consider some remarks made by Paul Ramsey[7] on this matter of pursuit. Ramsey, in trying to justify "direct" killings of the fetus to save the mother, argues as follows:

> ... precisely the fact and the effects of *material* aggression of life upon life should be the main concern in our attempts to penetrate the meaning of the Christian life, not waiting to find a guilty aggressor before we are permitted ever to take one life in order to save another in a mortal conflict of lives and values. Just so, in warfare it is not guilty aggressors but material aggression that ever warrants the taking of life to stop the action that is going on.

Ramsey is surely correct in insisting that it is not necessary that an aggressor (or pursuer) be guilty in order that we be morally justified in taking his life to save the life of the pursued. This is precisely why we rejected the condition of guilt. But his theory of material aggression is incorrect. While it is not entirely clear what he means by "material aggression," his claim faces serious difficulties under a variety of interpretations. He may simply mean "poses a danger to." But if so, then material aggression does not justify killing the pursuer to save the life of the pursued. After all, the satisfaction of the condition of danger is not, as we have seen, sufficient to justify killing the pursuer. On the other hand, he may mean something stronger like "posing a danger to by performing some action or attempt." But while he would then be right in supposing that material aggression justified killing the pursuer, his point would have no relevance to the question of abortion. As we have seen, the fetus performs no such attempt or action. We conclude, therefore, that Ramsey's theory of material aggression is of no help in justifying abortion.

In short, then, the mother cannot justify aborting her fetus, even when its continued existence threatens her life, on the grounds that abortion is a permissible taking of the life of a pursuer.

1.2 A Permissible Case

I have used the traditional paradigm of the killing of the pursuer as the expression of an initial exception to our fundamental moral intuition that it is wrong to take the life of another human being. Are there any other cases in which it is permissible to take on life in order to save another? Let us again proceed by example, for it is example that calls forth the intuitive judgment that allows us to reach determinations about the delicate questions we are taking up here (and I shall implicitly be insisting that such intuitions are at the root of all our moral determinations, whether we are willing to admit it or not).

Example a.

By a series of actions for which no one is to blame, the two people in room r_2 and the one person in room r_1 will be blown up by a bomb. The only way to prevent the ignition of the bomb is to defuse it by destroying the triggering mechanism that is located in room r_1. Unfortunately, the person in r_1 will be destroyed along with the mechanism, and no way is known of destroying the mechanism without destroying him. He is, however, the only one who will die if the mechanism is destroyed; should nothing be done, all three people will die. Our intuition is that the triggering mechanism should be destroyed and the two lives saved, even though the life of the person in r_1 is taken as a result.

Example b.

A small village is surrounded by a hostile group of brigands who demand that the villagers kill Pietro, an innocent villager whose death the brigands seek. If the villagers do not kill Pietro, the brigands threaten to (and the villagers have every reason to believe that they will) destroy the village and everyone in it (including Pietro). The village is cut off from outside help and acceding to the demands of the brigands is the only way to save the inhabitants. Again, our intuition is that one ought to save the life of the villagers even if achieving that end does mean taking Pietro's life.

How are we to account for these cases? Why, in these cases, is it permissible (and perhaps even obligatory) to take the life of one person in order to save the lives of the others? These surely are not cases of killing a pursuer; only the condition of danger is met in either of them. At least three answers suggest themselves:

1. In these cases, the person whose life will be taken is going to die anyway as a result of the circumstances of the case. If his life is taken, however, the other lives will be saved. Taking his life is an optimal act, since no lives are sacrificed beyond those lost in the unaltered course of events, and some are gained. We may generalize that it is permissible to take B's life to save A's life if B is going to die anyway and taking B's life is the only way of saving A's life (we shall refer to this as the answer that nothing is lost). Note please that that is the essential condition, and that it is not necessary to the validity of this answer that more lives than A's be saved, so long as both A and B would have perished without intervention.

2. In these cases, it is a question of sacrificing one life to save not one life but many other lives. While the life to be sacrificed is as valuable as any other life, when we weigh all the lives that can be saved by that sacrifice, we find that the many lives outweigh arithmetically the one. There is, of course, something unsatisfactory about such calculations, but there is something even harsher about suffering the consequences of refusing to take responsible moral action. We may generalize that it is permissible to take B's life to save the lives of A and C if taking B's life is the only way of saving their lives (we shall refer to this as the answer that the number of lives saved should be maximized).

3. In these cases, the primary intent is certainly not to take the life of anyone; it is to save lives. The taking of life is an unintended although certainly foreseen consequence of a permissible (and perhaps even obligatory) action. In general, it is permissible to do an action that will result in the taking of A's life if you do not intend that result,

although it may be foreseen, and if the intended results outweigh this unfortunate unintended result (we shall refer to this as the answer that only intended consequences have validity in moral calculations).

The answer that only intended consequences have validity is based upon an important moral principle, one that has played a significant role in Roman Catholic moral thought for a long period of time. That is the principle of double effect. Consider a certain action A against the performance of which there is some absolute moral prohibition. Imagine, moreover, a case in which it is necessary to do some other action that, unfortunately, inevitably has the consequence of the performance of the action A. The performance of A is neither intended as an end nor as means to the acquisition of some end. It is an unintended but inevitable (and foreseen) side consequence of the performance of the second action. Then, according to the principle of double effect, providing that the benefits of the intended results outweigh the unfortunate unintended result, it is permissible to perform the action in question even though it means also doing the action A.

As an example of the application of this principle, let us take the bombing of innocent civilians as the absolute moral prohibition and imagine a case in which, in defending a country that has been unjustly attacked, it is necessary to bomb the enemy's rocket emplacements. Inevitably, certain innocent civilians who live nearby will be exposed to the effects of the attack, but bombing these civilians is intended neither as an end nor as a means to acquiring some end. Then, according to the principle of double effect, it would be permissible to bomb the rocket emplacements, providing that the good that action accomplishes (presumably in achieving a just victory) outweighs the evil results of the bombing of the innocent civilians.[8]

I suggest that the principle of double effect is open to serious question. To begin with, it presupposes that there is, conceptually, a distinction between what a person intends to do, whether as an end or as a means to an end, and what he does only as a foreseen inevitable consequence of the performance of some other action.[9] I believe,

moreover, that even if this distinction can be drawn, it does not
have the moral significance attributed to it. There are those who
claim[10] that the drawing of this distinction makes a difference in the
way in which we evaluate the person who performed the action in
question. If his performance of action A was intended, then he is
culpable in a way that the person whose performance of the action
A was unintended even if foreseen is not. It is possible to understand
the grounds of this conclusion, but our concern is with the evaluation
of actions and not with the evaluation of agents. We want to know
whether the fact that the performance of the action A in certain circumstances was unintended is significant to the moral permissibility of
doing the action whose inevitable consequence was the performance
of the action A. And it is very unclear as to why it should be.

There is, however, still a further problem here. The answer that only
intended consequences have validity is unhelpful in analyzing our
second case. When, in that case, the villagers take Pietro's life, that is
precisely what they intend to do as a means of saving their own lives,
and what we have is not merely an inevitable consequence of some
other action that they have performed. The principle of double effect
is too weak to serve here.

We turn then to our first two and more plausible answers. What is
the difference between them? The first says that, in the two cases we
considered, it is permissible to take someone's life because he will die
anyway. The second says that, in those cases, it is permissible to take
someone's life because doing that will result in the saving of the largest
possible number of lives. These two answers disagree about those cases
in which a person would survive if his life were not taken but the
taking of his life results in the saving of many other lives. The first
answer does not justify the taking of any life that would not be lost
by the inevitable operation of circumstance. According to our second
answer, however, it would be permissible, in such cases, to kill one
person in order to save the others, so long as the number saved is larger.
In that case, one would still be maximizing the number of lives saved.

Once this central distinction between these two answers is observed, one sees that the answer that the number of lives should be maximized is open to question. It has standard utilitarian overtones, and, like the utilitarian concept of the maximization of happiness, it asserts that the right action is the one that maximizes the number of human lives saved. I believe that it is unjust that the happiness of however many individuals should be brought about by causing suffering to a few, and all the more that it is unjust that life be preserved for many by being withdrawn from a few. The answer that nothing is lost, in contrast, is not open to such objections. It allows B's life to be taken only when not taking it will not make any difference, when B will die anyway. In such cases, B is not being treated unfairly, and if taking his life will save other lives, it is permissible (and perhaps even obligatory) to do so.

This point emerges even more clearly if we imagine the following two modifications of Examples a and b:

Example a'.

By a series of accidents for which no one is to blame, five people in room r_2 will be blown up by a bomb. The only way to prevent the ignition of the bomb is to defuse it be destroying the triggering mechanism that is located in room r_1, but the single person in room r_1 will be destroyed along with the mechanism. If nothing is done, that person in r_1 will survive.

Example b'.

A small village is surrounded by a hostile group of brigands who, desiring (for their own diabolic reasons) to compel the villagers to sacrifice an innocent man, demand that they kill Pietro. If the villagers do not kill Pietro, the brigands threaten to (and the villagers have every reason to believe that they will) kill all of the village leaders (among whom Pietro is *not* included). The village is cut off from outside help, and acceding to the brigands' demand is the only way to save the village leaders.

The important thing to note here is that, according to the maximization of numbers of lives answer, the triggering mechanism should still be destroyed and the villagers should still kill Pietro. After all, it is still a question of taking one life to save several others. But we have observed that the acts in question would be wrong because, when life is concerned, no majority can continue to exist by unjustly taking the life of a minority, in this case the man in r_1 and Pietro. It would seem, therefore, that the maximization of lives answer should be rejected and that the only one of our answers that is acceptable is (1), the answer that nothing is lost.

It might be claimed that we are introducing, in our objection to the maximization of lives principle, an unjustifiable asymmetry between the taking of lives and the saving of lives. After all, while I am concerned with the man whose life is about to be taken, have I not, it could be argued, been too little concerned with the men whose lives will be lost if I do not act?

I have indeed supposed that there is an asymmetry between the taking of lives and the saving of lives, but this supposition seems justified. Consider, once more, Case a'. If I destroy the triggering mechanism, then I will have acted in violation of a moral prohibition and will have *unjustly* violated my moral obligation to the person I have killed. But if I do not destroy the triggering mechanism, then not my action but the action of others or of circumstances will have resulted in their deaths. To be sure, I shall have failed to save their lives, but in those circumstances, I am not obliged to do so, and my failing to do so involves no unjust violation of my moral obligations to them.

In defending the asymmetry, I am assuming that, in cases like a' and b', the obligation to a person not to take his life is commanding even when it can be satisfied only by failing to save the lives of others, while the obligation toward a man to save his life does not have the same strength. But this is quite plausible; the obligation not to take a life is clearly of higher priority than the obligation to save lives and is present in a great many cases in which the latter is not. After all, while I am normally under an obligation to another person not to take his life even when my own life or my own well-being is at stake, I certainly am not normally under an obligation[11] to another person to save his life at the cost of my own life (or even at the cost of a significant impairment of my well-being).

All of this sheds light upon a certain problem raised by Bennett.[12] He questions the existence of a moral (but not of a conceptual) distinction between killing a person and merely refraining from saving that person's life. But that is a derivative distinction. The fundamental distinction is between the obligation not to take a person's life and the obligation to save a person's life. It is because the former is far stronger than the latter, and therefore nullifies the latter when the two conflict, that it is sometimes wrong to kill a person while permissible not to save another person.

Let us then agree to accept the nothing-is-lost principle[13] as an answer to the question why, in the cases that we are considering, it is permissible to take some lives to save others. How, still maintaining our assumption about fetal humanity, does that answer affect the problem of abortion? Its major effect[14] is to cause us to distinguish two types of cases in which some consider it desirable to abort the fetus to save the mother. In one type of case, if we do nothing, the fetus will survive and the mother will die. Such cases are, of course possible only at the end of pregnancy. In them, we ought not to abort the fetus, for taking its life to save the life of the mother is unfair. In the second type of case, if we do nothing, neither the mother nor the fetus will survive. In such a case, aborting the fetus is allowable.

We seem to have found one type of case in which, even if we assume that a fetus is a human being, it is permissible to abort the fetus to save the life of its mother. But our argument for this claim depends upon the accuracy of the nothing-is-lost principle. Since this principle is not unproblematic, we must turn to a further consideration of it.

1.3 Further Restrictions on a Permissible Case

Nothing is lost, as we say, only in the sense that no life is lost that would not have been lost in any case. But if we apply our principle, life is taken (even though it would otherwise have been lost by circumstance), and this taking may be unjustifiable murder despite the considerations that we have put forward. Moreover, one could easily imagine a variation of the examples we have employed, a variation in which the factor of time is much more significant than we have made it. Suppose there is a considerable amount of time between the taking and the losing that would have occurred had the taking not been done. What then?

Let us first discuss the idea of the taking of life as murder. Saint Thomas Aquinas, writing about a different case, enunciated a relevant point of view:[15] "Evils are not to be done that good may come from them . . . and therefore a man ought rather to let the infant perish/in hell/ than that he himself perish, committing the criminal sin of homicide in the mother." Is all killing homicide, or murder?

One may distinguish four ways of describing A's taking the life of $B:$ (1) A is taking B's life; (2) A is taking the life of an innocent man $B;$ (3) A is taking the life of an innocent man B, who is not pursuing $A;$ (4) A is murdering B. There clearly are cases in which (1) and, as we saw in Section 1.1, (2) are correct descriptions of an action but (4) is not. In some sense, the question that we considered in the last section was whether there could be circumstances in which (3) would be a correct description of the act but (4) would not. Certain commentators deny the possibility of making this distinction and flatly and without analysis construe the taking of any innocent nonpursuing life as murder. It seems to me that the preponderance of intuition is that that analysis ought to be made and that such killings are not necessarily equivalent to murder.

For a long time now, utilitarianism has reigned supreme in moral philosophy, and it is the utilitarian view that any action, even murder, must be evaluated in terms of its consequences. The implicit sense is that there may be cases in which favorable consequences justify the action in question. As for me, I am in agreement with those (like Anscombe[16] and Geach[17]) who maintain that there are some actions, like murder, that are never justified. Still, I believe that we can make useful nonutilitarian distinctions between the qualities of acts that seem similar or identical. If so, the question before us now is whether a particular action is correctly regarded as an act of murder, and that may lead to entirely different conclusions. Murder, I say, is the unjust killing of a human being. It is not merely the killing of an innocent human being, as our examination of the case of the pursuer showed. Now the question that we are considering is whether the taking of the life of any nonpursuer is always murder. My argument has been that it is not so, that there are some nonpursuers who may be killed without being murdered just because no injustice is being done to them since they are going to die anyway.

I must admit that in every circumstance conceivable in which one takes B's life to save A's life, B is going to die anyway. Death ultimately awaits all of us, and it is the end of any course of human events. So, as our principle now stands, it contains the dangerous implication that one can take a person's life whenever that is the only way of saving the life of another person, and this is clearly mistaken. Obviously, we need some stronger condition than "B is going to die anyway." The time has come to make explicit what in fact was implicit in some of our earlier arguments. In particular, two modifications of our earlier Answer 1 seem plausible:

($1'$) It is permissible to take B's life to save A's life if B is going to die anyway *in a relatively short time* and taking B's life is the only way of saving A's life (we shall refer to this as the principle that time counts).

($1''$) It is permissible to take B's life to save A's life if B is going to die anyway *by the same cause that would have killed A* and taking B's life is the only way of saving A's life (we shall refer to this as the principle that the cause counts).

Looking at our Examples a and b, we see how these modified principles work. The principle that time counts justifies killing the man in r_1 because he will die anyway within the near future, and it justifies killing Pietro because he will die anyway when (in the near future) the brigands destroy the village. The principle that the cause counts justifies killing the man in r_1, because, if nothing is done, he and the people in r_2 will all be killed by the bomb's explosion, and it

original principle affect the
rsion (1**) places even stronger
n life than does our original
y does not permit abortions that
ms of the original principle. But
according to the original nothing-
re not according to the final version.
, an abortion is always permissible
die if nothing is done and the only
rt the fetus. According to the final
le only if, in addition to the satisfaction
will die in a relatively short time if
re is no way to save the fetus or there is
dure, we have determined that we should
etus.

the conclusion of Mrs. Foot[19] about this

te, as it might be in the abortion case,
e one than none. Probably we should decide
n weighing her life against that of the
resting that, a few years later, we might
way.

trange about this remark. If one assumes, as
t the fetus already is, at the time in question,
y should there be this difference between the
and the fetus-mother decision? Perhaps the
as in mind comes when she talks about
e idea this suggests is that we are supposed to
e case in which we have to choose which of
ve (when, for example, we only have enough
to save one), and that we should there, and
lives and see which to save. Adopting this approach,
, for reasons still to be advanced, that the mother's
unts more.

justifies killing Pietro because, if nothing is done, he and all of the villagers will be killed by the brigands' destruction of the village. On the other hand, neither principle justifies the taking of the life of a human being to save the life of any other on the simple ground of the exchange of one life for another. Under ordinary circumstances, B is not going to die anyway in a relatively short period of time, and, if nothing is done, B's death (when he does eventually die) will have nothing causally to do with A's death.

In trying to decide about the validity of these principles, it will be helpful if we see more clearly the differences in their implications. A consideration of the following two modifications of one of our original cases helps to call out these differences:

Example a″.

By a series of accidents for which no one is to blame, the two people in room r_2 will be blown up by a bomb within a few minutes. The only way to prevent the ignition of the bomb is to defuse it by destroying the triggering mechanism which is located in room r_1, but the single person in room r_1 will be destroyed along with the mechanism. However, he is having a massive coronary attack and will certainly die anyway within the same range of time. The obvious differences here are the explicit introduction of the element of time and of separate cause (in the case of the person in r_1).

Example a‴

By a series of accidents for which no one is to blame, the two people in room r_2 will be blown up by a bomb within a few minutes. The only way to prevent the ignition of the bomb is to defuse it by destroying the triggering mechanism that is located in room r_1, but the single person in room r_1 will be destroyed along with the mechanism. If nothing is done, that person will be wounded by the general explosion of the bomb. Though he will eventually die as a result of the explosion, he will live on for a few years in apparent recovery. Here the element of time is presented in another variant.

The principle that time counts justifies killing the man in r_1 in Example $a″$ because he will die anyway in a relatively short time, but it does not justify killing the man in r_1 in Example a''' since he will live on for some years. The principle that the cause counts, on the other hand, justifies killing the man in r_1 in Example a''' since, if the triggering mechanism is not destroyed, his own death will eventually be caused by the same explosion that kills the people in r_2, but it does not justify killing the man in r_1 in Example a'', since, if nothing is done, his death will be caused by disease.

Which, if either, of these principles is correct? The whole rationale, in cases like the ones we are considering, for taking life to save other life is that the human being whose life is taken loses nothing of significance and is not therefore being treated unfairly. But if, as in Example a''', he will live for a significant length of time if we do nothing, our taking his life now means that we will have unfairly subjected him to a significant loss. Consequently, the whole rationale for the taking of lives in such cases collapses, and, in cases like Example a''', it is wrong to take that person's life. Since, however, the principle that the cause counts justifies killing the man in r_1 in Example a''', it is evidently mistaken.

The question of how long B is going to live without intervention is central to the question of whether his life may be taken to save A's. What we must now consider is whether any further condition plays a role; in particular, is the cause of B's death if we do nothing relevant in any case? To put the question another way, is the principle that time counts adequate, or must we add to it some additional condition, perhaps refined, that, if nothing is done, the same event will cause the death of A and B?

It is extremely difficult to answer this question. On the one hand, our intuition is that the cause is relevant. On the other hand, the powerful and plausible principle that nothing is lost would clearly justify taking the life of the man in r_1 even in Case a''. And since the whole justification for taking a human life in these cases is that nothing is lost by doing so, why should we be concerned with the cause? With some hesitation therefore I conclude that we should adopt the principle that the time counts as the commanding distinction.[18]

I find this approach objectionable for two reasons: (a) it is not at all obvious that this approach is superior to a random choice approach even in the case where we have to choose which life to save; (b) the case of an abortion is not a case of choosing which life to save but a case of choosing whether and whom to kill. Whatever we may decide about the difficult case of choosing which life to save, it seems that in our case (which involves killing someone) an injustice will be done to whomever you kill unless that person either cannot be saved or has a fair (just) chance to be saved. It is for these reasons that I reject Mrs. Foot's approach in favor of the one suggested by applying the final version of the nothing-is-lost principle.

Let us see then where we stand. We have found two types of cases in which it would be permissible to take the life of a human being to save the lives of other human beings. The first, the case of the pursuer, is not applicable to cases of abortion even when the continued existence of the fetus threatens the life of the mother. The second, the case where nothing is lost, is applicable in a few cases of abortion. As no other type of case suggests itself, we shall tentatively conclude that these are the only cases in which it is permissible to take the life of a human being to save the life of another human being. And we shall also therefore tentatively conclude that if there is some point in fetal development after which the fetus is a human being, then from that point on the fact that the mother would die otherwise does not justify abortion unless the stringent requirements laid down in our final condition are met.

2 The Morality of Abortion (2)

In the previous chapter, I compared an abortion to save the life of the mother to other cases in which it is permissible to destroy one life to save another. It may be objected that that is precisely what is wrong with my analysis—that there are special conditions of the mother-fetus relation in general, or particular instances of that relation, that make it morally permissible for the mother to abort the fetus even after it is a human being. In this chapter, I will address some such conditions commonly cited in justification of abortion.

2.1. The Woman's Right to Her Body

It is a common claim that a woman ought to be in control of what happens to her body to the greatest extent possible, that she ought to be able to use her body in ways that she wants to and refrain from using it in ways that she does not want to. This right is particularly pressed where certain uses of her body have deep and lasting effects upon the character of her life, personal, social, and economic. Therefore, it is argued, a woman should be free either to carry her fetus to term, thereby using her body to support it, or to abort the fetus, thereby not using her body for that purpose.

In some contexts in which this argument is advanced, it is clear that it is not addressed to the issue of the morality of abortion at all. Rather, it is made in opposition to laws against abortion on the ground that the choice to abort or not is a moral decision that should belong only to the mother. But that specific direction of the argument is irrelevant to our present purposes; I will consider it in Chapter 3, when I deal with the issues raised by laws prohibiting abortions. For the moment, I am concerned solely with the use of this principle as a putative ground tending to show the permissibility of abortion, with the claim that because it is the woman's body that carries the fetus and upon which the fetus depends, she has certain rights to abort the fetus that no one else may have.

We may begin by remarking that it is obviously correct that, as carrier of the fetus, the mother has it within her power to choose whether or not to abort the fetus. And, as an autonomous and responsible agent, she must make this choice. But let us notice that this in no way entails either that whatever choice she makes is morally right or that no one else has the right to evaluate the decision that she makes. It is, of course, just this type of evaluation of moral decisions that we have been making in Chapter 1.

In short, our sole and appropriate concern is with the following issue: Should we modify the conclusions we reached in Chapter 1, so as to allow some (or all) abortions as morally permissible, on the ground that a woman ought to be free to do what is necessary to retain control over her body?

At first glance, it would seem that this argument cannot be used by anyone who supposes, as we do for the moment, that there is a point in fetal development from which time on the fetus is a human being. After all, people do not have the right to do anything whatsoever that may be necessary for them to retain control over the uses of their bodies. In particular, it would seem wrong for them to kill another human being in order to do so.

In a recent article,[1] Professor Judith Thomson has, in effect, argued that this simple view is mistaken. How does Professor Thomson defend her claim that the mother has a right to abort the fetus, even if it is a human being, whether or not her life is threatened and whether or not she has consented to the act of intercourse in which the fetus is conceived? At one point,[2] discussing just the case in which the mother's life is threatened, she makes the following suggestion:

In [abortion], there are only two people involved, one whose life is threatened and one who threatens it. Both are innocent: the one who is threatened is not threatened because of any fault, the one who threatens does not threaten because of any fault. For this reason, we may feel that we bystanders cannot intervene. But the person threatened can.

But surely this description is equally applicable to the following case: A and B are adrift on a lifeboat, B has a disease that he can survive, but

A, if he contracts it, will die, and the only way that *A* can avoid that is by killing *B* and pushing him overboard. Surely, *A* has no right to do this. So there must be some special reason why the mother has, if she does, the right to abort the fetus.

There is, to be sure, an important difference between our lifeboat case and abortion, one that leads us to the heart of Professor Thomson's argument. In the case that we envisaged, both *A* and *B* have equal rights to be in the lifeboat, but the mother's body is hers and not the fetus's, and she has first rights to its use. The primacy of these rights allow an abortion whether or not her life is threatened. Professor Thomson summarizes this argument in the following way:[3]

I am arguing only that having a right to life does not guarantee having either a right to be given the use of, or a right to be allowed continued use of, another person's body—even if one needs it for life itself.

One part of this claim is clearly correct. I have no duty to *X* to save *X*'s life by giving him the use of my body (or my life savings, or the only home I have, and so on), and *X* has no right, even to save his life, to any of those things. Thus, the fetus conceived in the laboratory that will perish unless it is implanted into a woman's body has in fact no right to any woman's body. But this portion of the claim is irrelevant to the abortion issue, for in abortion of the fetus that is a human being the mother must kill *X* to get back the sole use of her body, and that is an entirely different matter.

This point can also be put as follows: as we saw in Chapter 1, we must distinguish the taking of *X*'s life from the saving of *X*'s life, even if we assume that one has a duty not to do the former and to do the latter. Now that latter duty, if it exists at all, is much weaker than the first duty; many circumstances may relieve us from the latter duty that will not relieve us from the former one. Thus, I am certainly relieved from my duty to save *X*'s life by the fact that fulfilling it means the loss of my life savings. It may be noble for me to save *X*'s life at the cost of everything I have, but I certainly have no duty to do that. And the same observation may be made about cases in which I can save *X*'s life by giving him the use of my body for an extended period of time. However, I am not relieved of my duty not to take X's life by the fact that fulfilling it means the loss of everything I have and not even by the fact that fulfilling it means the loss of my life. As our discussion in Chapter 1 showed, something more is required before rights like self-defense become applicable. A fortiori, it would seem that I am not relieved of the duty not to take life by the fact that its fulfillment means that some other person, who is innocently occupying my body, continues to do so.

At one point in her paper,[4] Professor Thomson does consider this objection. She has previously imagined the following case: a famous violinist, who is dying from a kidney ailment, has been, without your consent, plugged into you for a period of time so that his body can use your kidneys:

Some people are rather stricter about the right to life. In their view, it does not include the right to be given anything, but amounts to, and only to, the right not to be killed by anybody. But here a related difficulty arises. If everybody is to refrain from killing that violinist, then everybody must refrain from doing a great many different sorts of things . . . everybody must refrain from unplugging you from him. But does he have a right against everybody that they shall refrain from unplugging you from him? To refrain from doing this is to allow him to continue to use your kidneys . . . certainly the violinist has no right against you that you shall allow him to continue to use your kidneys.

Applying this argument to the case of abortion, we can see that Professor Thomson's argument would run as follows:

a. Assume that the fetus's right to life includes the right not to be killed by the woman carrying him.

b. But to refrain from killing the fetus is to allow him the continued use of the woman's body.

c. So our first assumption entails that the fetus's right to life includes the right to the continued use of the woman's body.

d. But we all grant that the fetus does not have the right to the continued use of the woman's body.

e. Therefore, the fetus's right to life cannot include the right not to be killed by the woman in question.

And it is also now clear what is wrong with this argument. When we granted that the fetus has no right to the continued use of the woman's body, all that we meant was the he does not have this right merely because the continued use saves his life. But, of course, there may be other reasons why he has this right. One would be that the only way to take the use of the woman's body away from the fetus is by killing him, and that is something that neither she nor we have the right to do. So, I submit, the way in which Assumption d is true is irrelevant, and cannot be used by Professor Thomson, for Assumption d is true only in cases where the saving of the life of the fetus is at stake and not in cases where the taking of his life is at stake.

I conclude therefore that Professor Thomson has not established the truth of her claims about abortion, primarily because she has not sufficiently attended to the distinction between our duty to save X's life and our duty not to take it. Once one attends to that distinction, it would seem that the mother, in order to regain control over her body, has no right to abort the fetus from the point at which it becomes a human being.

It may also be useful to say a few words about the larger and less rigorous context of the argument that the woman has a right to her own body. It is surely true that one way in which women have been oppressed is by their being denied authority over their own bodies. But it seems to me that, as the struggle is carried on for meaningful amelioration of such oppression, it ought not to be carried so far that it violates the steady responsibilities all people have to one another. Parents may not desert their children, one class may not oppress another, one race or nation may not exploit another. For parents, powerful groups in society, races or nations in ascendancy, there are penalties for refraining from these wrong actions, but those penalties can in no way be taken as the justification for such wrong actions. Similarly, if the fetus is a human being, the penalty of carrying it cannot, I believe, be used as the justification for destroying it.

2.2. The Mother as Creator

There is a second set of considerations that could be raised in favor of the claim that the mother occupies a special status vis-à-vis the fetus, a status that permits abortion even if the fetus has a full right to life and even when the life of the mother is not at stake. These have to do with the idea that the fetus is an entity that owes its existence to the mother.

One way of stating the argument is the following: the fetus has come into existence only because of the mother's act of intercourse, and it therefore owes its life to the mother. If so, the continued existence of the fetus cannot be allowed to work a hardship upon the mother, and she has a right to terminate its existence by aborting it. What she once gave, she may now withdraw.

There are several reasons for being suspicious about this argument. To begin with, a similar argument could be advanced for infanticide and even for killing one's thirty-year-old child. To be sure, one might modify the principle in question by emphasizing the fact that the continued existence of the fetus, as well as its having come into existence, depends upon the mother. That is, currency of the mother's support may be made a condition of the withdrawal of that support. But even that modified principle would permit infanticide where the infant can survive only by the mother's feeding it (imagine a case in which the mother's feeding it is the only available source of nourishment).

There is, moreover, a second difficulty with this argument, namely, that it presupposes that the mother's bringing the fetus into existence gives her a special right to harm the fetus, so long as her own interest is served, a right that other individuals do not of course have. This assumption is not new in the history of mankind. It is the principle that lay behind all those legal systems that allowed parents to sell the child into slavery or to take its life for financial benefit or convenience. Now we still think that parents have certain special rights over their children (especially their infant children) that others do not have, or do not have in the same way and to the same extent. These include

the rights to punish the child, to make decisions about how it is to be
educated, about the religious faith in which it is raised, and so forth.
But the central assumption is that these rights are exercised for the
benefit of the child. Discipline is meant to keep the child from harming
itself or to socialize it, education to increase its awareness of the world
and of itself, religious training to form its moral and religious behavior.
As far as I can see, we have given up the idea that parents have the
right to punish, educate, or exhort the child in a way that harms it,
though they may benefit thereby. But it is just this objectionable type
of right that this argument presupposes, so the argument should be
rejected.

Is there any element of truth in the argument we are considering?
It does suggest one interesting point. Suppose someone has risked his
life to bring you into existence or maintain your existence, and suppose
that you can now save his life by giving up yours. Do you have an
obligation to him to do so? I can imagine an affirmative answer to this
question, although I must confess that I would not make it myself.
Even, however, if the obligation exists, it cannot be concluded from
such a case that the mother has the right to take the life of the fetus
since (a) that would be a case of the forcible taking of life as opposed
to the voluntary sacrificing of it, and (b) the mother can only rarely
be accurately said to have risked her life to bring the fetus into existence
or to have risked her life to keep it in existence.

Similar points can be made about a second version of this argument:
if the mother had done nothing at all, then the fetus would not have
come into existence. If, therefore, she aborts the fetus, he is not going
to be in any worse state than he would have been if the mother had
done nothing.

Once more, this argument would justify infanticide as well as abortion. Moreover, it is based upon the dubious principle that what one
is given (in this case, life) may later be taken on the grounds that it
was a gift in the first place. Many gifts, to the contrary, must be
regarded as irrevocable, and I suspect that that is all the more so when
what is given is something touching central human values.

In short, the mere fact that the mother has brought the fetus into existence and continues to maintain it in its existence gives her no right to abort the fetus. Indeed, quite the opposite argument may be made. It is possible that the mother has a special obligation to preserve rather than to harm the fetus precisely because she has brought the fetus into existence. After all, it is a valid intuition that parents have special obligations to make certain sacrifices for their children. But I propose letting that issue go for now, since considering it would raise all types of issues about our special obligations to our children that lie beyond the scope of this essay.

2.3. Abortions for the Sake of the Child

There is still a third set of considerations that is often appealed to in support of the claim that abortion is different from the ordinary taking of human life. These considerations have their foundation in what is thought to be the consequences of unwanted birth. Should the mother want an abortion, the fetus, if nevertheless brought to term, would be an unwanted child, and, so the argument goes, it would therefore be better if the fetus were not brought to term but were aborted. Here, presumably, it is the psychological effect upon the child that is the justification. In the same circumstances, the argument may be carried one step further and the effects of the psychologically damaged child upon society may become the rationale for abortion. Presumably, such a child will not be personally stable and that lack of stability will manifest itself in antisocial behavior. Carrying the argument one step further, appeal will be made to the effects upon the physical welfare of the child born into a poor family, perhaps already carrying the burden of several other children, or into no family at all, and to the effects of such a birth upon the family: the other children, the mother, the father. Not only may such a child be denied an adequate provision for its sustenance and shelter, for its training and education, but its existence may deprive, in effect, others of these advantages as well.

There are, then, two sets of arguments, one psychological and the

other physical, and in each, one argument focuses on the welfare of
the child himself and the other on the welfare of society. As an instance
of the first kind of argument, that having to do with the welfare of
the child, let me quote the following passage from a letter to the
New York Times:[5]

If the Right to Life advocates were on a campaign for an improvement
in the quality rather than the quantity of life, so that the world might
truly be a beautiful place to be born into and it could realistically be
assumed that every fetus would want to be born and live, then I would
be willing to listen to their arguments on the "right to be born." Until
that time, however, I think they should consider the possibility that
their actions might impose the "burden of being born" on many
unwitting and unwilling fetuses for whom life in the world as it is
would be far from a right to be protected.

As the last sentence makes clear, this is an argument based upon
considering what is best for the fetus, and, as such, it is comparable to
arguments commonly made in favor of euthanasia. That is obviously a
comparison that Daniel Callahan[6] had in mind when he raised the
following objection to this argument:

While one could easily grant, under a number of circumstances, a
"right to die," it becomes a very strangely exercised right when the
being in question has it exercised on its behalf by others.

  Some distinctions may usefully be made at this point about the
"right to die":
A. An individual has the right, in at least some cases (those in which
it is for his benefit), to stop others from taking extraordinary measures
to keep him alive.
B. An individual has the right, in at least some cases (in which it is for
his benefit), to take his own life.
C. An individual has the right, in at least some cases (in which it is for
his benefit), to ask others to take his life for him, and they then acquire
the right to do so.
D. An individual's life can be taken by others in at least some of the

cases covered under C though the individual does not make such a request (because he is unable to do so).

About Claim A, there is a strongly favorable intuitive consensus.[7] Claim B raises the issue of the morality of suicide. Claim C extends that right to commit suicide so that the individual who is, for one reason or another, unable to perform the act, can ask others to do it for him. Claim D is, of course, the most questionable claim.

Returning now to the Callahan objection, we see that it is profoundly ambiguous. Is Callahan, in the first clause conceding Claim A or B? And is he, in the second, challenging Claim C or D? Moreover, whatever he is doing, is he right in challenging the move from the claim he concedes to the claim he challenges?

Let us suppose that he is conceding Claim B. It is difficult, after all, to imagine the grounds for anything but acceptance. Can one justifiably move from Claim B to C and D, or is Callahan right in objecting to either (or both) of these moves?

The following argument would seem to justify the move from Claim B to C: If a man has a right to do something without obtaining the consent of others, then he has a right to ask others to do it for him, and they have the right to do it. After all, why should he be prevented from exercizing his rights just because it is inconvenient or impossible for him to exercise them alone? So, given Claim B, Claim C follows.

What about the move from Claim C to D? Let us imagine that a person has a right to do something and that his exercising that right would be highly advantageous for him. Let us also imagine that he is so incapacitated that he is neither able to exercise that right nor to ask someone else to do it for him. And let us finally imagine that we have certain knowledge that the person would exercise the right or would appoint someone else to do so if he could. Then, although no one may have the obligation to help the person in question by exercising the right for him, it would seem permissible for others to do so as his unappointed agents.[8] So, providing that we may assume that someone else can be sure of the appropriate facts, Claim D seems to follow from C in at least some of the cases that C covers.

In short, then, providing that we are willing to accept the assumptions involved in the preceding arguments, the move from B to D can be justified, and we can reject Callahan's objection. We turn then to a direct consideration of this argument for abortion. It is as follows:
1. Because the mother does not want to bear this fetus, it is to the fetus's advantage that he not be born, that his life be taken by abortion.
2. This case falls under Claim D, and the mother is therefore justified in aborting the fetus.
The question that we must consider is whether this is a good argument.

The truth of the first premise is highly debatable. What we can say for sure about the unwanted fetus is that there is a good probability that he will be an unwanted child (but only a good probability, since the mother may find that her feelings change when he is born) and that there is a good (but lesser) probability that he will consequently suffer. But it is, I think, an excessive reach from these observations to Argument 1, partially because there remains a real possibility that the events described will not materialize and partially because it is very uncertain that the harm that will result will be so great that it would have been to the fetus's advantage that he not be born at all. Argument 1 becomes even more implausible when we keep in mind the possibility of the mother's giving the fetus up for adoption after it is born. When we come to consider Argument 2, the argument fails entirely. If our argument for Claim D is correct, then one could use it to justify an abortion only if one could be sure that the fetus, if it could think the issues out, would elect to be aborted. The unpredictability of an unknown future makes this assumption impossible, and I conclude, therefore, that while Callahan's objection fails, an abortion cannot be justified on the grounds that it is for the benefit of the fetus.

But what about the second kind of argument? What about arguing for abortion on the grounds that the social damage caused by unwanted children is sufficient to justify abortions? Though I will consider the effect of the unwanted child on the family in detail later, let me say for now that this argument is even less plausible. To argue this way is to argue for avoiding a possible social problem by taking a life. In an age where we doubt the justice of capital punishment even for very dangerous criminals, killing a fetus who has not done any harm, to avoid a future problem it may pose, seems totally unjust. There are indeed many social problems that could be erased simply by destroying those persons who constitute or cause them, but that is a solution repugnant to the values of society itself.

In short, then, if the fetus is a human being, the appeal to its being unwanted justifies no abortions.

2.4. The Model Penal Code Cases

All of the arguments that we have looked at so far are attempts to show that there is something special about abortion that justifies its being treated differently from other cases of the taking of human life. We shall now consider claims that are confined to certain special cases of abortion: the case in which the mother has been raped, the case in which bearing the child would be harmful to her health, and the case in which having the child may cause a problem for the rest of her family (the latter case is a particular case of the societal argument). In addressing these issues, we shall see whether there is any point to the permissibility of abortions in some of the cases covered by the Model Penal Code[9] proposals.

When the expectant mother has conceived after being raped, there are two different sorts of considerations that might support the claim that she has the right to take the life of the fetus. They are the following: (A) the woman in question has already suffered immensely from the act of rape and the physical and/or psychological aftereffects of that act. It would be particularly unjust, the argument runs, for her to have to live through an unwanted pregnancy owing to that act of rape. Therefore, even if we are at a stage at which the fetus is a human being, the mother has the right to abort it; (B) the fetus in question has no right to be in that woman. It was put there as a result of an act of aggression upon her by the rapist, and its continued presence is an act of aggression against the mother. She has a right to repel that aggression by aborting the fetus.

The first argument is very compelling. We can all agree that a terrible injustice has been committed on the woman who is raped. The question that we have to consider, however, is whether it follows that it is morally permissible for her to abort the fetus. We must make that consideration reflecting that, however unjust the act of rape, it was not the fetus who committed or commissioned it. The injustice of the act, then, should in no way impinge upon the rights of the fetus, for it is innocent. What remains is the initial misfortune of the mother (and the injustice of her having to pass through the pregnancy, and, further, to assume responsibility of at least giving the child over for adoption or assuming the burden of its care). However unfortunate that circumstance, however unjust, the misfortune and the injustice are not sufficient cause to justify the taking of the life of an innocent human being as a means of mitigation.

It is at this point that Argument B comes in, for its whole point is that the fetus, by its mere presence in the mother, is committing an act of aggression against her, one over and above the one committed by the rapist, and one that the mother has a right to repel by abortion. But we saw in the previous chapter that (1) the fetus is certainly innocent (in the sense of not responsible) for any act of aggression against the mother and that (2) the mere presence of the fetus in the mother, no matter how unfortunate for her, does not constitute an act of aggression by the fetus against the mother. Argument B fails then at just that point at which Argument A needs its support, and we can therefore conclude that the fact that pregnancy is the result of rape does not give the mother the right to abort the fetus.

We turn next to the case in which the continued existence of the fetus would threaten the mental and/or physical health but not necessarily the life of the mother. Again, we saw in the previous chapter that the fact that the fetus's continued existence poses a threat to the life of the mother does not justify her aborting it. It would seem to be true, a fortiori, that the fact that the fetus's continued existence poses a threat to the mental and/or physical health of the mother does not justify her aborting it either.

We come finally to those cases in which the continuation of the pregnancy would cause serious problems for the rest of the family. There are a variety of cases that we have to consider here together. Perhaps the health of the mother will be affected in such a way that she cannot function effectively as a wife and mother during, or even after, the pregnancy. Or perhaps the expenses incurred as a result of the pregnancy would be utterly beyond the financial resources of the family. The important point is that the continuation of the pregnancy raises a serious problem for other innocent people involved besides the mother and the fetus, and it may be argued that the mother has the right to abort the fetus to avoid that problem.

By now, the difficulties with this argument should be apparent. We have seen earlier that the mere fact that the continued existence of the fetus threatens to harm the mother does not, by itself, justify the aborting of the fetus. Why should anything be changed by the fact that the threatened harm will accrue to the other members of the family and not to the mother? Of course, it would be different if the fetus were committing an act of aggression against the other members of the family. But, once more, this is certainly not the case.

We conclude, therefore, that none of these special circumstances justifies an abortion from that point at which the fetus is a human being.

2.5. Callahan on the Sanctity of Life

One final set of remarks seems to be in order. Throughout the previous two chapters, we have been arguing that the assumption that the fetus is a human being entails certain moral conclusions prohibiting the performance of abortions. These arguments rest upon certain assumptions about what we may, and may not, do to a human being. These assumptions about the very limited conditions under which we can take the life of a human being are assumptions about the sanctity of human life.

In his recent and fundamental book on this topic, Daniel Callahan has argued that one cannot derive from the assumption of the sanctity of human life any absolute prohibitions against taking the life of the fetus (even assuming the strongest possible assumptions about the humanity of the fetus). He[10] puts his point as follows:

> A major objection worth levelling at any rigidly restrictive moral code on abortion is that it is prone to hold that an absolute prohibition of induced abortion is a logical entailment of "the sanctity of life." The logical route leading to this prohibition is that "the sanctity of life" means and can only mean under all circumstances that bodily life is to be preserved, which in turn is taken to entail a prohibition of the taking of fetal life. No room is left, in this deductive chain, for a recognition of other demands of the principle.

The point that Callahan makes is, in outline, sound. He is claiming that there is no way that one can infer an absolute prohibition against the taking of human life from the premise that life is sacred. One cannot infer this because there may be other obligations, obligations that are also part of what we mean by the sanctity of life, that outweigh the obligation not to take a person's life in a given case.

It is not clear how far Callahan's point can be pushed. In the last two chapters, where we have explored the question of the conditions under which the obligation not to take the life of a human being can be overridden, we found that there are in fact very few cases of that sort. And only one of these cases seemed relevant to the issue of abortion. We found only one case in which an abortion would be permissible. So Callahan's point, while quite right abstractly, sheds very little light on the issue of abortion. It remains for Callahan to suggest cases relevant to the issue of abortion in which this obligation not to take the life of a human being can be overridden.

The closest that Callahan comes to doing so is in the following passage:[11]

> As suggested, the claim of the individual's "right to life" as the pre-eminent rule seems well founded. Yet it is clearly conceivable that this right and the attendant rules protecting it could come into question (as they have on occasion in the past) if the survival of the species or of a whole people or nation were in danger from overpopulation, a scarcity of medical facilities, or in time of war. . . . The abandonment

of the elderly in earlier Eskimo culture as well as the practice of infanticide in a variety of earlier societies testify to the extreme pressures which can be placed upon communal survival. To see such practices only as an instance of a primitive insensitivity to human life would be to show a lack of imagination about the desperate straits in which a community could find itself.

Two comments are in order here: (1) Callahan's examples are not to the point. In his two examples, a society was forced, by virtue of a threat to its very existence, to abandon its obligations to care for the helpless. The result of the abandonment of this obligation is, of course, the deaths of the helpless, but it would surely be incorrect to say that the communities in question took the lives of those helpless people. There are, no doubt, cases in which abandoning someone is equivalent to taking his life, but this is so only when there exists an obligation to care for the persons in question that has not been overridden; (2) Far more important, none of the cases in question seems relevant to the issue of abortion. The closest we come to relevance is when Callahan refers to the threat to the survival of a society by overpopulation. But we do have alternative methods (and ones that are surely morally far more preferable) for meeting the problems of overpopulation. Birth control, and not abortion, is surely the solution to those problems.

In short, then, while Callahan is correct in reminding us that the obligation not to take a life may be overridden, he has failed to give us any cases in which it should be overridden that are relevant to the abortion issue. And in our examination of possible cases, we found only one. While that is no ultimate proof—there may be, after all, cases and considerations that we have not yet thought of—that we found but one such case does suggest that we were right in concluding that this aspect of the sanctity of life is so significant that it leaves an extremely circumscribed field in which abortion is morally permissible.

3 Abortion and the Law

Many people who are opposed to abortion under certain circumstances, on the ground that in such circumstances abortion is the unjustifiable taking of the life of a human being, maintain nevertheless that it is wrong (or, at least, inappropriate) for the state to legislate against abortion. These are the people who feel that there should be different answers to the moral and legal questions about abortion. In this chapter, we shall assess their claim.

Such a claim cannot, of course, be considered without also considering the more general question of when it is right (or appropriate) for the state to legislate against any action. That, of course, is a fundamental issue that is independently worthy of study, quite apart from its relevance to our present preoccupation.

3.1. Morality and Legality

The claim that we shall consider consists of the joint assertion:

Principle 1. It is under certain circumstances wrong for X to perform an abortion upon Y, even when X is a licenced physician and Y a consenting mother (who may also have the consent of the father) because this act is under such circumstances the unjustifiable taking of a human life, that is, murder.

Principle 2. It is wrong (or at least inappropriate) for the state in current circumstances to prohibit such abortions by law, and they should therefore be or remain legal.

These two claims are not, by themselves, incompatible. But it is possible that there is a correct principle about what type of wrong actions ought to be proscribed by law that, conjoined to these two claims, yields an inconsistent triad. If so, then the position we are considering is indefensible. But is it correct? What is the principle?

One principle that would be sufficient is as follows:

Principle 3. It is right (or appropriate) for the state to prohibit by law any action that is wrong.

This principle seems questionable for two reasons. To begin with, it implies that such a law ought to exist even if the wrong action produces no bad consequences, or at least none for anyone but the person who is doing the action. The idea of a crime without a victim casts familiar doubts upon Principle 3. But even more significantly, Principle 3 leaves out the whole question as to whether legal means are always the right (or appropriate) ones for discouraging or preventing the performance of a wrong action. Would it be right to pass a law prohibiting such an action if, because of special circumstances in the case at hand, the existence of the law would increase the frequency of the performance of that wrong action? Or would it be right to pass a law prohibiting such an action if, because of special circumstances in the case at hand, the existence of the law has subsidiary effects more damaging than the continued performance of the wrong action?

Much more plausible than Principle 3 is another principle, also sufficient:

Principle 4. It is right (or appropriate) for the state to prohibit by law any wrong action that results in harmful consequences for someone other than the performer of the action (or anyone else who has voluntarily consented to his doing the action). Principle 4 is much more plausible than 3 because it avoids the issue of crimes without victims. Principle 4 rules out the claim we are considering because it, the principle that abortion is murder but it should nevertheless be or remain legal, and certain additional very plausible assumptions (the fetus does not consent to the abortion, and the taking of a human life is an action that has bad consequences for the person whose life is being taken) do form an inconsistent set of propositions. The trouble with Principle 4, however, is that it does not avoid the second objection against 3. Even if the wrong action does have these bad consequences, it may still be wrong (or inappropriate) to prohibit that action by law. After all, the existence of the law may, because of special circumstances in the case at hand, still increase the frequency of performance of the wrong action or produce very undesirable subsidiary effects.

A similar problem arises even for the very plausible principle:

Principle 5. It is right (or appropriate) for the state to prohibit by law any action that involves the unjustifiable taking of human life.
This principle and the principles that abortion is murder but nevertheless should be or remain legal do form an inconsistent triad. But one cannot consent to the general claim made in Principle 5. We should still insist that the existence of the law may, because of special circumstances in the case at hand, increase the frequency of performance of the wrong action or produce subsidiary effects of overriding importance (like the loss of even more human lives).

What rapidly emerges from this type of consideration is the conviction that questions about the rightness (or appropriateness) of laws prohibiting certain actions cannot be settled by decisions about the rightness or wrongness of the actions themselves or even by coupling such decisions with decisions about why the actions are wrong. I believe that conviction to be correct even in the extreme case in which an action is wrong because it is the unjustifiable taking of a human life.

We are now in a position to see that there is no simple objection on the grounds of inconsistency to the joint assertion of the claims that abortion is murder but should nevertheless be or remain legal. Such an objection would require some true principle of the form "It is right (or appropriate) for the state to have a law prohibiting any action of type A" (where abortion, if it is the unjustifiable taking of a human life, would necessarily be of the type in question). But we have observed that all principles of this form are wrong, and we must thus admit that this variety of challenge is not sustainable. In examining the question of whether there should be laws against abortion, therefore, we must go beyond the moral examination of abortion to consider the consequences of such laws in a given society.

3.2. Law and Society in a Democracy
Before turning to such considerations, however, we must first examine several important assertions about law and society that, if true, would justify the joint assertion of the principles that abortion is murder but nevertheless should be or remain legal. The first is the assertion that

citizens of a pluralistic society must forgo the use of the law as a method of enforcing what are their private moralities. It might well be argued that in our pluralistic society in which there are serious disagreements about the status of the fetus and about the rightness and wrongness of abortion in consequence, it would be wrong (or inappropriate) to legislate against abortion.

Such assertions about a pluralistic society are difficult to evaluate because of their imprecision. So let us first try to formulate some version of them more carefully. Consider the following general principle: Principle 6. When the citizens of a society strongly disagree about the rightness and wrongness of a given action, and a considerable number think that such an action is right (or, at least, permissible), then it is wrong (or inappropriate) for that society to prohibit that action by law, even if the majority of citizens believe such an action to be wrong.

There are a variety of arguments that can be offered in support of the principle. One appeals to the right of the minority to follow its own conscience rather than being compelled to follow the conscience of the majority. That right has a theoretical political justification, but it also is practically implicit in the inappropriateness in the members of the majority imposing this kind of enforcement upon the minority that would be opposed were they the minority and were the enforcement being imposed upon them. Another argument appeals to the detrimental consequences to a society of the sense on the part of a significant minority that the law is being used by the majority to coerce. Such considerations make it seem that a principle like 6 is true.

If Principle 6 is true, it is easy to offer a defense of the joint assertion of the principles that abortion is murder but nevertheless should be or remain legal. All we need are the additional obvious assumptions that the citizens of our society strongly disagree about the morality of abortion and that at least a significant minority of individuals believe that there are many cases in which abortion is permissible. From these assumptions and Principle 6 it follows that abortions should be or remain legal even if they are murders.

The trouble with this argument is that it depends upon Principle 6.

I agree that, because of the considerations mentioned already, something like Principle 6 must be true. But Principle 6 as formulated is much too broad to be defensible. Consider, after all, a society in which a significant number of citizens think that it is morally permissible, and perhaps even obligatory, to kill Blacks or Jews, for example, because they are seen as being something less than fully human. It would seem to follow from Principle 6 that the law should not prohibit such actions. Surely this consequence of Principle 6 is wrong. Even if a pluralistic society should forgo passing many laws out of deference to the views of those who think that the actions that would thereby be prevented are not wrong, there remain some cases in which the force of the law should be applied because of the evil of the actions it is intended to prevent. If such actions produce very harmful results and infringe upon the rights of a sufficiently large number of individuals, then the possible benefits that may be derived from passing and enforcing a law preventing those actions may well override the rights of the minority (or even of the majority) to follow its conscience.[1]

Principle 6 must therefore be modified as follows:

Principle 7. When the citizens of a society strongly disagree about the rightness and wrongness of a given action, and a considerable number think that such an action is right (or, at least, permissible), then it is wrong (or inappropriate) for that society to prohibit that action by law, even if the majority of citizens believe such an action to be wrong, unless the action in question is so evil that the desirability of legal prohibition outweighs the desirability of granting to the minority the right to follow its own conscience.

Principle 7 is, of course, rather vague. In particular, its last clause needs further clarification. But Principle 7 is clear enough for us to see that it cannot be used to justify the joint assertibility of the principles that abortion is murder but should nevertheless be or remain legal. Principle 7, conjoined with the obvious truths that the citizens of our society strongly disagree about the rightness and wrongness of abortion and that a significant number of citizens believe that, in certain circumstances, the right (or, at least, a permissible) thing to do is to

have an abortion, does not yield the conclusion that abortion should
be or remain legal if abortion is murder. After all, if abortion is murder,
then the action in question is the unjustifiable taking of a human life
and may well fall under the last clause of Principle 7. The destruction
of a fetus may not be unlike the killing of a Black or Jew. They may all
be cases of the unjust taking of a human life.

I turn to another point that has indirectly been made in my earlier
discussion of Principles 6 and 7. They both are constructed to deal
with the cases in which it is the majority which thinks that the action
in question is wrong and the only question before the majority is
whether to grant the minority, which presumably believes that the
action is right (or permissible), the opportunity to follow its conscience. There is of course another circumstance, to which I have
earlier referred, to consider, that in which the majority thinks that the
action in question is right (or at least permissible) while only a minority
believes such an action is wrong. This may, indeed, be the situation
with respect to abortion in America today. Imagine that the minority
has enough political power to obtain or continue legislation that
prohibits the action in question. Perhaps there is a principle like 6 that
deals with a case like this and may justify the joint assertion of the
principles that abortion is murder but should nevertheless be or remain
legal.

What would such a principle look like? The following formulation
suggests itself:
Principle 6'. When the citizens of a society strongly disagree about the
rightness or wrongness of a given action, and a majority thinks that
such an action is right (or, at least, permissible), then it is wrong (or
inappropriate) for that society to prohibit that action by law, and it is
wrong (or inappropriate) for the minority who believes that such an
action is wrong to use its political power to obtain such a law or to
retain such legislation if already in effect.
The problem is that Principle 6' faces the same difficulties that Principle 6 faced. If the action in question is so wrong (and infringes on
such significant rights) according to the minority conception, and if

the existence of the law could really prevent a great deal of evil from being done, then the possible benefits from preventing this evil by passing and enforcing laws against such actions may well override the rights even of the majority to follow its conscience. So one has to give up Principle 6′ and move to a modified version of Principle 7, and it will be of no more help than was Principle 7. In short, then, nothing is gained by taking into account the fact that it is only a minority that believes that the action in question is wrong.

An adequate account of the relation between law and morality in a pluralistic society does not therefore easily support the joint assertion of the principles that abortion is murder but should nevertheless be or remain legal. Even in a pluralistic society, there are occasions in which a minority and even a majority should be prevented from following its conscience. The case of abortion, for the adherents of the principle that abortion is murder, is a prime example of just such an instance.

A second principle about law and society that may serve to justify the joint assertion of the principles that abortion is murder but should nevertheless be or remain legal is suggested in the following argument by Roger Wertheimer:[2]

The existence and powers of the state are legitimated through their rational acceptability to the citizenry, and it would be irrational for the citizens to grant to the state any coercive power whose exercise could not be rationally justified to them. Thus, the state has the burden of proving that its actions are legitimate. Now, without question, the present abortion laws seriously restrict the freedom and diminish the welfare of the citizenry. A law with that effect is not *ipso facto* unjust, but the state has the burden of showing that such a law is necessary to attain the legitimate ends of the state. But the social costs of the present abortion laws are so drastic that only the preservation of human lives could justify them. So to justify those laws the state must demonstrate that the fetus is a human being. But if that can't be done at all, the state can't do it either, so the laws must be deemed an unjustifiable burden and hence an illegitimate exercise of power.

Essential to this argument is the assumption that it is impossible to demonstrate (and perhaps even to make it seem likely, for surely the requirement that one demonstrate that the law is justified is too strong) to the citizenry that the fetus is a human being. Let us grant it for now, so that the discussion can proceed, although it is the purpose of the second part of this book to suggest that that claim is false.

Three principles may be drawn from Wertheimer's argument: Principle 8'. No law is justified unless the state can demonstrate (or perhaps just make probable the claim) to the citizenry that it is necessary (or perhaps just the best way) to attain the legitimate ends of the state.

Principle 8''. No law that restricts the freedom of the citizens of the state is justified unless the state can demonstrate (or perhaps just make probable the claim) to the citizenry that it is necessary (or perhaps just the best way) to attain the legitimate ends of the state, ends that are sufficiently important to justify the restrictions imposed by that law.

Principle 8'''. No law that restricts the freedom of the citizens of the state and diminishes their welfare is justified unless the state can demonstrate (or perhaps just make probable the claim) to the citizenry that it is necessary (or perhaps just the best way) to attain the legitimate ends of the state, ends that are sufficiently important to justify the restrictions and the diminution imposed by the law.

We need not now decide which of these three versions is preferable, nor whether any is reducible to the others, for there is a straightforward objection that applies to all of them. Imagine a group of people who believe that Blacks or Jews, for example, ought to be destroyed, want very much to destroy Blacks or Jews, and feel strongly that their rights are infringed when the law prevents them from doing so. Let us say that they have this belief by religious conviction. Could it be demonstrated *to those individuals* that the law in question is necessary to meet the legitimate needs of the state? As revelation is involved here, let us say that it cannot. And if it cannot, should that prohibition be removed?

We can put the issue more directly: Wertheimer fails to understand that the point he makes about the abortion dispute can be made with regard to many other critical issues as well. Many times the majority has certain values (based perhaps upon religious and metaphysical views) that are so different from those held by some minority that it cannot prove *to the minority* that laws enforcing those values are justifiable (it can, of course, prove it to the satisfaction of the majority). We would surely not want to rule out the use of the law in all of those cases. All that we should say is that the majority, as far as possible, should respect the views of the minority. But how far is "as far as possible"? That question is, of course, the question of how to behave in a pluralistic society, and we have already read what has to be written about it.

I conclude, therefore, that Wertheimer's principles lead us back to our principles about legislation in a pluralistic society, and that none of his principles justifies holding that abortion should be or remain legal even though it is murder.

A third principle about law and society that might be used to try to justify the joint assertibility of the principles that abortion is murder but nevertheless should be or remain legal is offered by Daniel Callahan:[3]

Even if it can be argued that induced abortion is a form of murder . . . it is still necessary to show that this form of killing which is *sui generis* in being the killing of prenatal life does pose a threat to the common good . . . it seems to me that we cannot deny it [the woman's request for an abortion] unless two conditions are met: (1) that granting her this right would violate our consciences (and this would apply only to the doctor being asked to perform the abortion), or (2) that it would pose a threat to the peace, security, and safety of the whole society— that is, we, as citizens, would be harmed by granting such a right to women.

The principle that Callahan seems to be using here is as follows: Principle 9. When some members of a society feel that they have a right to do something, then the whole society ought to oppose it by legislation (as distinguished from individuals' opposing it by refusing to cooperate) only if that action poses a threat to the peace, security, and safety of the whole society.

At first sight, this seems strange. After all, if abortion is murder, the action in question certainly poses a threat to the peace, security, and safety of some members of the society, namely, the fetuses. What Callahan seems to have in mind, then, is that the action must pose a threat to the *whole* society. His reference to "the whole," if not meant perfectly literally—surely it would be sufficient if the threat were directed against most members—is meant very seriously.

But even when we see what he has in mind, his claim is still very strange. Why should not the law be used to protect some members of society from having their rights violated by other members of society? Why can that protection be extended only if the violation of rights poses a threat to the peace, security, and safety of the whole society? Principle 9 seems to lack any persuasive rationale and should, I submit, be rejected.

Still a final claim about law and society that might be used to justify the joint assertion of the principles that abortion is murder but should be or remain legal is raised by the following remarks[4] made in the report of the Commission on Population Growth and the American Future:

> In the development of western culture, the tendency has been toward a greater protection of life. At the same time, there is a deep commitment in our moral tradition to individual freedom. . . . The Commission believes that the various prohibitions against abortion throughout the United States stand as obstacles to the exercize of individual freedom: the freedom of women to make difficult moral choices based upon personal values, the freedom of women to control their own fertility, and finally, freedom from the burdens of unwanted childbearing.

This emphasis on the elimination of abortion laws as an important step in the liberation of women is particularly well brought out by Hardin:[5]

> Let us recall the underlying justification for all birth control practices: to keep women from a now needless form of slavery, to make a woman the master of her own body. The emancipation of women is not complete until women are free to avoid the pregnancies they do not want [by abortion].

As one compares these passages, one sees the following argument emerging: (a) women ought to be free to control their own fertility, to be the masters of their own bodies, to avoid unwanted childbearing; (b) laws prohibiting abortions interfere with the exercise of this freedom; (c) therefore, there should be no such laws. At first glance, this argument seems convincing. After all, who could challenge (a) or (b), and it certainly seems to follow from them that there should be no laws prohibiting abortions. So what is there to object to in this argument?

Further reflection reveals, however, that the argument in question rests upon a principle about laws in society that is not quite right. That abortions should be legal follows from (a) and (b) only if one adopts Principle 10:

Principle 10. No law ought to interfere in any way with the exercise of morally sanctioned freedoms.

The trouble is that Principle 10 is inadequate. Even if one ought to have a certain freedom, there may be some ways of exercising that freedom that are wrong because they interfere with the rights of others, and then there ought to be laws against those ways of exercising the freedom in question. Examples are legion. A person ought to be free to engage in the religious activities that he believes in. But regard for that freedom constitutes no reason for abolishing laws that prohibit certain actions (murder, for example) even when those actions are performed in a religious ceremony (human sacrifice, for example). Again, a person ought to be free to say what he wants. But that is no reason for abolishing laws that prohibit certain actions (libel, for example) even when those actions are performed because the person is saying what he wants to say.

There is, of course, another principle that somewhat resembles Principle 10 and is more plausible:

Principle 10'. No law ought to interfere with the exercise of a morally sanctioned freedom unless the performance of the action it prohibits interferes with the rights of others.[6]

This principle avoids the earlier objection, since it accommodates the law against murders performed in religious acts since these acts interfere with the rights of the victim. And it allows the law against libel, since libelous utterances interfere with the rights of whomever is libeled.

If, however, we adopt Principle 10' rather than Principle 10, the argument we are considering for the joint assertibility of the principles that abortion is murder but should nevertheless be or remain legal collapses. All that we can conclude is that there should be no laws prohibiting abortion unless abortion interferes with the rights of others. But if abortion is murder, it surely does. So those who believe that abortion is wrong because it is murder cannot use this argument to justify their claim that there should nevertheless be no law against abortion.

3.3. The Problems Raised by Antiabortion Statutes

Many arguments have commonly been offered in defense of the legalization of abortions performed by doctors upon consenting mothers. They include the following:

Argument 1. The only legitimate interest the state ever had in preventing abortions, the threat to the health of the mother, is no longer present because of the safety of modern abortion techniques. A good statement[7] of this argument follows:

There is little evidence of the legislative intent behind the nineteenth century anti-abortion laws enacted in this country. What evidence exists indicates the laws were enacted to protect the woman's health. If guarding the health of the woman from dangerous operations was the motivation for enacting the anti-abortion statutes, that reason no longer exists.

Argument 2. Laws prohibiting abortion are harmful to the practice of medicine because they lead to state intrusion into what should be a private relation between the doctor and his patient and because they prevent the doctor from practicing medicine as he sees fit. The dangers to the practice of medicine from these laws are well outlined in the following statement:[8]

Every patient must have an honest relation with her doctor if her doctor is to acquire the necessary information for proper diagnosis and treatment. The anti-abortion laws prevent the establishment of such a relation, for the patient who wants an abortion views her meeting with her doctor as an adversary proceeding. . . . When his patient asks for an abortion, the doctor must worry about the threat of criminal sanction. His diagnosis and treatment are clouded by the threat of prosecution. . . . In no area of medicine and surgery other than that of abortion does the State of California flatly prohibit the doctor or surgeon from prescribing or performing the treatment for his patient. . . .This edict is obviously an extreme invasion of the doctor's liberty to practice medicine in accordance with the best teachings and standards of the profession.

Argument 3. Abortion laws that allow abortions in only a few cases (for example, when necessary to save the life of the mother) are necessarily vague. They therefore result either in a doctor's not performing abortions when he should, in order to play safe, or in a doctor's having to gamble that the law will uphold his decision. In view of such considerations, many courts have been led to declare such laws unconstitutionally vague. A typical decision is as follows:[9]

We have concluded that the term "necessary to preserve" in section 274 of the Penal Code/the California abortion law/is not susceptible of a construction that does not violate legislative intent and that is sufficiently certain to satisfy due process requirements without improperly infringing on fundamental constitutional rights.

Argument 4. Abortion is a method of population control, and in view of our urgent population problem, we ought not to outlaw any method of population control.

Argument 5. Laws prohibiting abortion are commonly disregarded, and, like prohibition laws, their principal effect is to encourage a disrespect for the law.

Argument 6. Laws prohibiting abortions force pregnant women who need abortions to obtain illegal and unsafe abortions. Many deaths result, and much other harm to physical and mental health. This factor strongly influenced the Population Commission's recommendation to provide legal abortion on demand:[10]

The Commission regards the issue of illegal abortion with great concern and supports measures to bring this medical procedure from the backrooms to the hospitals and clinics of this country. It is becoming increasingly clear that, when abortion is available on request, one result is a reduction in the number of illegal abortions . . . A reduction in the number of illegal abortions has an important [downward] impact on maternal mortality.

Argument 7. Laws prohibiting abortion discriminate against the poor who can less often find the means of satisfying strict legal requirements or circumventing them altogether and obtaining safe, permissible abortions. This factor also influenced the decision of the Population Commission:[11]

Restrictive statutes also violate social justice, for when abortion is prohibited, women resort to illegal abortions to prevent unwanted births. Medically safe abortions have always been available to the wealthy, to those who could afford the high costs of physicians and trips abroad; but the poor woman has been forced to risk her life and health with folk remedies and disreputable practitioners.

We shall now see whether someone who believes that abortion is murder still may use certain of these arguments to defend the legalization of abortion. It is necessary to pose two questions: Are the premises of these arguments compatible with the claim that abortion is murder? And if so, and that claim can be annexed to them, does a good argument for legalizing abortion then remain, an argument of the form, "Although abortion is murder, there should be no law against abortion because. . . ."? If "yes" is the answer to both of these questions in connection with one or more of the arguments cited, then we shall have a good defense of the joint assertion of the principles that abortion is murder but should nevertheless be or remain legal.

A good example of an argument that cannot meet these tests is Argument 1. It is clear that one of its premises, the claim that the only interest the state has in abortions is in protecting the mother from a dangerous operation, is not compatible with the view that abortion is murder. If that is true, then surely the state, as part of its general role as a protector of human life, has an interest in prohibiting abortions to protect the life of the fetus.

The premises of Argument 1 are incompatible with the claim that abortion is murder. And when that claim is conjoined to the premises of Argument 4, the resulting statement, though consistent, is not the basis for a sound argument for legal abortion. Methods of population control are of course essential, but there are many means of reducing the surplus population, to use that phrase, that are undoubtedly effective but nevertheless morally repugnant. We would not, for example, allow infanticide or the execution of randomly selected adults as methods of population control, and, if abortion is murder, it should no more be allowed than those other methods.

Argument 2 is like Argument 4. Although we may be inclined to grant that a doctor should be free to practice medicine as he sees fit and that the doctor-patient relation should be a private one, and although these claims are compatible with the claim that abortion is murder, the argument fails when we conjoin that claim to the original premises. If abortion is murder, then the offense is so great that one cannot justify omitting legal prohibition as a means of preserving the rights of the doctor and the privacy of the doctor-patient relationship. Some limitations must be placed upon all rights, and certainly the most obvious purpose of such limitation is to save human life.

Argument 3 has a special type of shortcoming. It presupposes that any abortion law will contain some exceptions allowing limited legal abortion on specific grounds. It then goes on to argue that such an allowance will necessarily make any such law unfairly (and in the context of American law, unconstitutionally) vague, and concludes that all abortions should therefore be legal. But if, when the fetus becomes a human being, abortion is murder, why should any exceptions be allowed? Moreover, should such exceptions be regarded as necessary (rightly or wrongly), it is obviously illogical to claim that all limitations should be removed simply to avoid legal ambiguity. It would seem more reasonable to tolerate the ambiguity (as we tolerate, for example, ambiguities in what constitutes legitimate freedom of the press), or, if we feel drawn to an absolute view, to prevent abortion altogether.

It therefore seems to me that Arguments 1 through 9 cannot be used by partisans of the claim that abortion is murder to support the legalization of abortion. But these are clearly the weaker arguments, although they are often used. The far stronger arguments are 5 through 7. All these deal with the damaging consequences of the unavailability of legal abortions; they are, therefore, the types of argument that are likeliest to support the joint assertion of our two principles. We turn therefore to a consideration of them.

Let us begin with Argument 5. It should be noted at the outset that this argument in many of its forms is susceptible to serious overstatement of the claim that the main result of existing abortion laws is a disrespect for the law. It surely is the case that a good many contemplated abortions would not be carried out if they were illegal, even though a significant percentage would be carried out despite their illegality.

There are two ways of supporting this claim. The first is to note its intuitive plausibility. As long as abortion is illegal, there are many who will not proceed to obtain abortions because of the expense of an illegal procedure or because of their fear about its safety; these women will presumably proceed if abortion is legal. Moreover, if abortion is legal, the resulting element of social approval will certainly influence some women who would otherwise hesitate about having an abortion because they are unsure of its morality.

Second, there is indirect evidence to support this supposition. There have been studies[12] (conducted in Sweden and Hungary) of the subsequent histories of women who applied for a legal abortion and were refused one. Only a third to a half went on to obtain an illegal abortion. If, of course, no law had regulated abortion, all of these women would have proceeded. Again, while the evidence is mixed,[13] the preponderance indicates that when there is a significant liberalization of the abortion laws, at least a moderate drop in the birthrate follows. The implication is that many women who did not have illegal abortions do obtain legal ones.

Naturally, none of this evidence is conclusive, but it does make it plausible to suppose that the legalization of abortion in America will result in a significant increase in the number of abortions actually performed. In other words, the existence of abortion laws would reduce significantly the number of abortions actually performed.[14]

What therefore, Argument 5 really asserts is that the disrespect for the law engendered by abortion laws is so great and poses such a problem that abortions should be or remain legal even if the result is a significant increase in the number of abortions actually performed. The question we must now consider is whether one can still press this argument if abortion is murder. I am inclined to say that one cannot. After all, laws prohibiting abortions would, if abortions are murder, prevent thousands of additional murders every year. It seems hard to believe that the problem of disrespect for the law produced by antiabortion legislation is so great that we must pay this drastic price to circumvent it. The situation would be very different, of course, if Argument 5 were literally true and few, if any, abortions were prevented by their being illegal—but that seems highly unlikely.

Argument 5 derives much of its plausibility, I suppose, from the comparison with prohibition. The comparison is not a good one. We feel that prohibition of the manufacture, sale, and transportation of alcoholic beverages attempted to solve a social problem at much too great a price in terms of disrespect for the law because we feel that the only problem with drinking is excessive drinking. Although that is a serious problem, it is surely far less serious than the problem posed by abortion if abortion is murder. Moreover, it is at least possible that the prohibition laws actually had the effect of increasing the number of alcoholics, but the laws prohibiting abortion will not, on the evidence available to us, have the effect of increasing the number of abortions.

Argument 6 is, in a way, the strongest of the arguments. It claims that we must reject laws prohibiting abortion so as to prevent women who nevertheless seek abortions from being killed or injured by unqualified practitioners employing inadequate facilities. It would seem that the sanctity of human life compels us to oppose antiabortion laws. But I am afraid that even this argument loses its power if we grant that abortion is murder. If that view is correct, the argument becomes one that calls upon us to legalize abortion so that, by increasing the number of human lives taken by abortionists, we can save the lives of some of those people, mothers, guilty of the offense of unjustifiably taking (personally or by proxy) human lives. Surely, if abortion is murder, the innocent lives (of the fetuses) should take precedence over the lives of those (the mothers) who would take them. And since the number of human lives saved would probably be greater if abortion laws existed, then this argument is invalid.

We are left with Argument 7. As a claim about the hypocrisy of society, it is significant. There are far too many people who oppose (or do not seek) "liberalized" abortion laws because they know that statutes preventing abortion will leave them undisturbed—they are wealthy or influential enough to be able to obtain safe abortions whatever the law may demand. But as a reason for legal abortion, Argument 7 is insignificant. It is arguing that, since there is an inequality about who is allowed to go scot-free for murder, we should allow everyone to be completely exonerated for it. The obvious alternative to be pursued, even if it is difficult to achieve, is the abolishment of this inequality by allowing no one to go without penalty. In any case, the imperfection of government in achieving equality under the law should not be transformed into an argument for equal rights to murder.

3.4. Drinan's Argument

There is one final argument of a very different nature that we must consider. It is based upon the legal situation in the United States before the recent Supreme Court decisions concerning abortion. At that time, many state legislatures were considering proposals to "liberalize" antiabortion laws by allowing abortions under certain specific circumstances. Such proposals either followed or were heavily influenced by the Model Penal Code recommendations discussed in Chapter 2. From the point of view of the adherents of the thesis that abortion is murder, new statutes of that kind constituted state pronouncements that it is permissible to take innocent human lives in those circumstances. And since these laws generally allowed for abortion when the fetus was likely to be born defective, it was as though the legislature were saying that certain defective human lives have no value. All of this led some adherents of the view that abortion is murder to the conclusion that it would be better to have no laws regulating abortion rather than these "liberal" laws. If there were no laws, then the state would at least not be condoning acts of murder and denigrating the value of certain human lives.[15]

This argument may be reduced by steps to the following statements:
Step 1. Abortion is the unjustifiable taking of a human life, and, as such, it is always wrong.
Step 2. Under current circumstances, two possibilities alone may exist: either there will be no laws preventing abortion or there will be the Model Penal Code "liberal" laws.
Step 3. The former possibility is to be preferred to the latter; then, at least, the state will not explicitly condone the taking of human lives.
Step 4. Therefore, in the circumstances we find ourselves in now, there should be no laws prohibiting abortion.

This argument has one major advantage over all the others that we have been considering. It is the only argument that depends essentially on the truth of the claim that abortion is murder. All the other arguments were of the form, "Despite the fact that abortion is murder, there should be no laws prohibiting abortion because . . ." The form of this one is, "Owing to the fact that abortion is murder, we should have no laws prohibiting it because . . ."

The trouble with this argument is its Step 3. Step 3 does, indeed, point to an advantage of having no antiabortion laws in the current circumstances. But this is not enough. What have to be considered as well are the disadvantages of having no such laws, and there is one major disadvantage. It may be surmised that there are persons seeking abortions whose abortions would not be legal even under the "liberal" laws and who might not therefore obtain an abortion were "liberal" laws in force. Liberal abortion laws would therefore tend to save some (perhaps even many) lives that would be lost were there no laws at all, and surely that must take precedence over the desire to keep the state from condoning the taking of those lives. It should be noted, moreover, that the elimination of abortion laws would probably be viewed by most people as evidence that the state condoned all abortions and not as the maintenance by the state of a standard of neutrality on the issue of abortion.

3.5. The Argument for Legal Prohibition

Let me end by saying a few words about how the problem now stands. We have considered the possibility of arguing that abortion should be or remain legal even if abortion is murder and have found no sound argument for this position. What conclusions follow?

In order to answer that question, it is necessary for us to return to the principles about the relation between morality and legislation with which we began this chapter. There were two objections that we raised against the principles stated there. One, the problem of crimes without victims, is a problem that arose only for Principle 3, but it is one compelling enough to suggest that we are not going to be able to repair Principle 3. The other is the problem that arose because of the fact that the law is not always the appropriate means for discouraging and/or preventing the performance of any action. This objection can be taken to all of the principles, but I believe that the remaining principles can be modified so as to avoid the objection and to lead us to some conclusion about whether there should be laws prohibiting abortion.

Imagine some action that is morally wrong because it leads to bad consequences for someone other than the person who performs the action (or someone else who voluntarily consents to the performance of the action). Or imagine some action that is wrong because it involves the taking of a human life. Why should not there be a law prohibiting such an action? Surely one of the main functions of the state, through its legal system, is to prevent us from being harmed or killed by others. What we saw in the first section of this chapter is that there can in fact be reasons why no such law should be passed. The passage of the law may, we saw, lead in some circumstances to an increase in the number of such actions performed, or its enforcement may be achieved only at an unacceptable cost to the rights and welfare of others. But the important point to note is that there must be a good reason why the law in question should not be passed.

This point can also be put as follows. While we saw reasons to reject Principles 4 and 5, these reasons are not applicable to the following modifications of them:

Principle 4'. Unless there are special circumstances that would indicate otherwise, the state ought to prohibit by law any wrong action that results in harmful consequences to someone other than the performer of the action (or anyone else who has voluntarily consented to his doing the action).

and

Principle 5'. Unless there are special circumstances that would indicate otherwise, the state ought to prohibit by law any wrong action that involves the unjustifiable taking of a human life.

Moreover, both Principles 4' and 5' seem plausible. If the criminal law has any function at all, surely that function is to prevent us from being harmed or killed. If, therefore, there are no special circumstances arguing strongly against the law in question, the law seems desirable.

Assuming then that we adopt either Principle 4' or Principle 5', we can see that there should be laws prohibiting abortion if we assume that abortion is murder. After all, given that claim and either Principle 4' or Principle 5', we can infer that unless there are special circumstances present that would indicate otherwise, the state ought to prohibit abortion by law. And in light of the results of this chapter, in which we have examined all the special circumstances that are normally appealed to and found them wanting, we can tentatively conclude that if abortion is murder there should be a law prohibiting it.

Before ending, I would like to add just one word about what type of law that should be. It is often claimed that those who adopt the position advocated in this chapter should also conclude that abortion should be dealt with as a specific instance of the general legal prohibition of homicide. There is something theoretically attractive about the suggestion that there should be no law particular to abortion but merely a legal declaration that the taking of the life of the fetus is to be dealt with just like the taking of the life of any other human being. And if we believe that abortion is murder, this approach seems to express exactly what we believe.

Nevertheless, there are other considerations that suggest that there be special laws, with special penalties, covering abortion. To begin with, in light of the widespread feeling that abortion is not homicide, there is a real possibility that district attorneys will refuse to prosecute and juries refuse to convict in abortion cases if they were covered by the homicide laws. Moreover, in light of the fact that many of those who obtain abortions feel that what they are doing is morally permissive, it may be desirable to legislate different penalties for them.

There are then a variety of considerations that may lead to different conclusions about what a law prohibiting abortion should be like. But we need not consider this question now. It is sufficient for our purposes to conclude that, if abortion is murder, the state, in the circumstances we find ourselves in now, ought to have laws prohibiting abortion.

Part II

4 The Role of Human Reaction and Decision

In the first three chapters of this book, we have considered the implications of the assumption that there is some point in fetal development beyond which the fetus is a human being. We have seen that this assumption has substantial consequences for the moral and legal issues surrounding the abortion question. The time has now come, however, to see whether that assumption is true, and if it is, what that point of fetal development is beyond which the fetus is a human being.

Opinions differ greatly on this issue. There are those who deny that the fetus, before birth, is ever a human being. At the other extreme are those who claim that the fetus becomes a human being at the moment of conception. And there are, of course, many intermediary positions.

There is one presupposition that all of these positions have in common. It is that there is an objectively correct answer to this question, one that holds regardless of diversity of personal opinion and feeling. But not all moralists concede the truth of this presupposition. Some claim that whether or not the fetus is a human being depends, at least in part, upon certain subjective decisions involving it made by, and/or certain subjective reactions to it experienced by, other human beings. It is this claim that we shall consider in this chapter.

4.1. The Vagueness of "living human being"

It is a truism of the philosophy of language that many general terms, terms used to denote more than one object, are characterized by a certain vagueness and that there normally are cases, for which the philosophical term is "borderline cases," in which it is unclear whether the term in question is applicable to the given object. This unclarity is owing, not to a lack of knowledge about the object in question, but to an indeterminacy in the meaning of the term. As an example, consider the term "boat," which is defined in my dictionary as "a small open oared or sailing vessel." There is no problem about whether or not any one of a certain variety of objects on the lake is a boat.

But is the rubber raft to which a child has attached a makeshift sail a boat? Is the floating log he may paddle for his amusement? The answer to these questions is not very clear.

Why do general terms have this intrinsic vagueness? There are at least two causes, the first present in some cases and the second in others:[1]
1. The term has, as the criterion for its application, a set of conditions to be satisfied, but it is not specified how many of them must be satisfied. When some, but not all, of these conditions are satisfied, it is then unclear whether the term is applicable.
2. The term has, as the criterion for its application, the condition that it is applicable to cases that resemble certain standard cases. When situations arise in which there is a certain amount but not a perfect resemblance to the standard cases, it is unclear whether the term is applicable.

What ought one to do about this vagueness? Another truism of the philosophy of language is that one should not normally do anything. As long as the vagueness raises no practical problems, there is no reason to do anything about it. When, however, this vagueness raises practical problems, then some decision has to be made that will resolve it. The important thing to remember about such decisions is that they are neither true nor false. They are merely decisions resolving the vagueness in a given case. Thus, in our case, if the child is operating his raft on a lake and there is a rule against the use of boats on that lake, the question of whether the raft is a boat becomes a practical issue requiring solution. But there is no true answer, no correct answer, to the question. All that is involved in any such resolution is a decision to employ the term so as to cover, or fail to cover, the object under study.

The example that we have looked at is not a very important one. But the phenomenon that it illustrates is common, and there is no reason why it cannot arise in far more serious circumstances. Indeed, it may be suggested that this is what has happened in the case of the fetus. The term "human being," it may be suggested, is vague. There are entities (you, me) to which it is clearly applicable, and there are entities (a stone, a horse) to which it clearly is not. There are, however, some entities that are borderline cases. One such entity is the fetus. There is then, it may be claimed, no correct answer to the question whether the fetus is part of the denotation of "human being." What is called for is a decision whether we are going to use the term "human being" so that the fetus is part of its denotation or whether we will employ the term in such a way as to exclude the fetus from its denotation.

A natural concern that would arise, were we to adopt this approach, would be the identity of the decision makers. Is this a decision to be made by mother, father, and physician, by the community of those who speak the language, by all people? Is it one that must be made by a majority, by still a larger proportion of those making it, by all of them in agreement? The answer to these questions is not immediately evident.

There is, however, a far more fundamental objection to the analogy between the case of the rubber raft and the case of the fetus. In the case of the raft, the practical issue arises because of the existence of some regulation prohibiting the use of boats on the lake, a regulation that employs the term "boat." Because of the way such regulations are formulated and applied, the prohibition applies to some entity precisely because it can be regarded as among the denotation of the term "boat." So in that case, our question really is about the denotation of the term "boat." But in the case of the fetus, no analogous regulation exists, and our question whether the fetus is a human being is really about whether it has, independent of the denotation of "human being," certain natural and inherent rights.

There is another way of making essentially the same point. Imagine that there were no such phrase in the English language as "human being." Then there could, of course, be no question of whether the fetus is part of its denotation. But that would not mean that the question we raise about the humanity of the fetus would not exist. It would still be a real and serious question. So our question is not about the denotation of that term and cannot be resolved by some

decision about its denotation. That is, our question is a moral and not
a linguistic question. It is a question about whether certain entities
have certain rights, and decisions about the application of a term
cannot resolve it.

4.2. Deciding upon the Criterion of Humanity

Perhaps we have been too quick to dismiss the view that what is called
for is a decision. To be sure, no decision about the meaning of any
term will suffice. But perhaps what is required is some decision about
whether or not the fetus should be accorded the rights of a human
being?

Something like this seems to be the position of John O'Connor.
O'Connor agrees that once the criterion for humanity (for having the
rights of a human being) is settled, the question of the humanity of a
fetus is a purely scientific one. He claims, however, that it is we who
have to decide the criterion of humanity, and, therefore, in an indirect
way, it is we who ultimately have to make the decisions that will
determine whether the fetus has the rights of a human being:[2]

I suggest that the fundamental defect in Noonan's account is his
assumption that the criterion of humanity needs to be discovered.
Rather I suggest that we must *decide* what the criterion is to be.

In another passage, O'Connor puts his point as follows:[3]

It is possible to agree with Noonan that, in a sense, it is certainly an
objective matter whether or not a being is human, but point out that
it becomes objective only when human beings have decided what the
criterion of humanity is.

A variety of objections may be raised against this view. The one that
we should consider first is that it leaves the matter of human rights
open to arbitrariness and prejudice. After all, there are many imperfec-
tions in individual perceptions of what is or is not required to be a
human being. There are undoubtedly those who would claim that
certain minorities fail to meet fully the criterion of humanity. If a
vast majority entertains a prejudice against redheads and if that prej-

udice is reflected in a decision to specify nonredheadedness as one
of the necessary conditions for being a human being, does it follow,
as O'Connor's position seems to entail, that redheads have no right as
human beings? Of course not.

O'Connor is doubtless aware of this objection, and he comments upon
it as follows: "This is not, of course, to say that it is a subjective matter.
Rather, there are good and bad reasons for deciding in the way we
do."[4] Two questions naturally arise in response to such a remark:
(1) What is the basis for distinguishing between good and bad
reasons for such decisions and for distinguishing between good
and bad decisions? (2) And is that basis such that it does not also serve
as a basis for distinguishing between the one objectively correct and
all other incorrect answers to the question of what the criterion is to
be for being a human being. It is extremely important that O'Connor
be able to say "no" in response to this second question. If he cannot,
then he will have avoided the subjectivism he recognizes as dangerous
only at the cost of giving up his idea that the criterion of humanity is
a matter subject to decision (in the special way that word is used) and
at the cost of adopting our position that there is in fact one objectively
correct answer to the moral question, "When is an entity a human
being?"

Let us look at O'Connor's theory of good reasons and bad reasons:[5]

The reason that humanity is of interest to a person concerned with the
moral status of abortion is that he wants a way to decide the scope of
the moral principle to the effect that the taking of human life is wrong.
Hence humanity should be characterized in terms of those features
which are in fact related to the moral sensibility of human beings. . . . It
would do little good to couch the criterion of humanity in such a way
that the moral judgements we now make concerning human beings
would be felt to have no moral force when applied to the "newly
qualified" humans, whose humanity was first recognized only by the
new criterion of humanity.

This theory is very unsatisfactory because it fails to meet the original
objection. In a highly prejudiced society that has incorporated its

prejudices into its criterion of humanity, the only good criterion of humanity, according to O'Connor, will retain these prejudicial features. If we try to drop them out, so as to extend human rights to the minority in question, our new criterion of humanity will be unsatisfactory, according to O'Connor, since it is not related to the moral sensibility of the human beings in that society. Going back once more to the case of the redheads who in their society are not viewed as human beings, one would have to say, according to O'Connor, that it would be a bad decision to omit nonredheadedness as a criterion of humanity.[6]

Moreover, the reason that O'Connor gives for adopting his theory of good and bad decisions is not very convincing. To be sure, if one's decision extends the rules about human rights to entities not generally recognized as human beings, there is a chance that the rules will be broken in connection with these entities. In that sense, then, such a decision "would do little good." But given the force of law, the extension would stand some chance of holding. Further, it could have an educational effect (by making people think again about whether this minority is human), and could, all else aside, serve as an important statement of principle. It is not at all clear, then, that such a decision would be a bad one. Moreover, the mere fact that a correct decision will not have the desired consequences should not, by itself, be allowed to subvert it.

In short, then, O'Connor's way of distinguishing good from bad decisions will not do, partially because it does not solve the problem raised by prejudiced individual perceptions and partially because the reasons for it are unconvincing. Still, it has called our attention to the possibility of meeting our original objection to the decisional approach to the criterion of humanity. We still may find some other way of distinguishing good from bad decisions, or good reasons for making a decision from bad ones, a way that rules out as irrelevant the bad decisions (or decisions based upon bad reasons) about the criterion of humanity made on the basis of prejudiced judgment, while keeping as relevant the good decisions (or those made for good reasons). But at the moment that is only a possibility, for no such way has so far been discussed.

There is a second objection against the whole decisional approach that must also be considered. According to this approach, the criterion of humanity is determined by a decision. Whose decision? The answer that O'Connor seems to offer is that it is our decision, it is a decision that we human beings make. But, lacking a criterion of humanity, what sort of answer is that?

Let us put this point another way. Imagine that you have no idea as to what it is to be a human being. Would it help you then to be told that something is a human being if it meets the criterion of humanity to be decided upon by other human beings? Of course not. But is not this same circularity to be found in the views of the decisional approach?

There seems to be a possible reply to this objection. The situation we are in may not be like the situation described in the preceding paragraph. It is not true that we have no idea as to what it is to be a human being. Rather, there are many cases in which there is no confusion about what is or is not a human being, and we have a great deal of knowledge about what it is to be human. It is merely that there are some remaining cases that are unclear, and what we use to decide them are the criteria of humanity decided upon by those who clearly are human beings.

But is this reply really satisfactory? Does not it simply come down to the following: the criterion of humanity is to be decided upon by those clearly recognizable as human beings. And if this reply does, then the question naturally arises, "recognizable by whom?"

We can put this point another way. The reply makes the interesting suggestion that we need a decision about the criterion of humanity to deal specifically with a certain number of cases. There are many cases in which no decision is called for. And the decision about these unclear cases is to be made by those many human beings whose humanity can be ascertained independently of the decision about the criterion of humanity. So far, so good. But the reply gets into trouble by identify-

ing those human beings who are to make the decision on the basis of
the clear recognition that they are human beings. This is no good, for
the circularity reappears at this point.

I can see only one way for the decisional approach to avoid these
problems. It is to formulate its position as follows: there is a criterion
for humanity, and by applying it we can tell in some cases that the
entity in question is a human being and we can tell in other cases that
it is not. But there are some cases in which our criterion does not help
us, no matter how much information about that case we collect. What
are needed are some decisions about how to extend the criterion of
humanity to deal with those cases. These decisions are to be made by
those who are human beings according to the initial criterion. If this
is how the decisional approach is to be preserved, however, a key
supposition must be that there is an acceptable but incomplete criterion
of humanity. Since none seems immediately in the offing, we have here
once more a possible position rather than a position.

I conclude, therefore, that O'Connor's version of the decisional
approach (and, indeed, the whole decisional approach) is acceptable
only if the following stringent set of conditions can be met: (1) there
is a current criterion that identifies some entities as human beings
but leaves the question of the humanity of others unanswered; (2) there
are possible modifications of that criterion that would resolve these
open questions; (3) there is a basis for distinguishing good from bad
reasons for adopting a decision about how to modify the criterion or
for distinguishing good from bad decisions, but this basis is not a basis
for distinguishing a single objectively correct decision; (4) this basis
is justifiable and avoids the problem raised by prejudiced judgment
and the decisions that may follow from it.

4.3. The Social Policy Approach

Let us now consider another version of the decisional approach, one
that is popular among those who approach moral issues from the point
of view of social theory. An appropriate decision about the criterion
of humanity or the humanity of some particular entity, according to

this version, is one that makes reference to the societal implications of the decision and attempts, in light of these implications, to increase human happiness.

This approach is sometimes confined, in the area of inquiry that interests us, to decisions as to whether abortion should be prohibited by law, whether fetuses should be given the legal protection provided for human beings. But it might equally well, and sometimes seems to, be intended as an approach to the question of the moral permissibility of abortion, which depends very much indeed on decisions about humanity. We shall consider this approach as a theory intended to deal with both of these issues.

To see how this approach functions, we can consider the following statement[7] by Glanville Williams, in which he comments on the idea of taking the fetus to be human from the moment of conception:

If the line is to be drawn by reference to social considerations and human happiness, then pretty obviously the time of impregnation is the wrong one to take.

Why? Because such a decision would, for example, inflict a great deal of suffering upon mothers who respect it and would produce all the social problems caused by unwanted children. So, the argument goes, while we do have to make a decision about when the fetus becomes a human being and while there is no one objectively correct such decision, we can say that the decision that the fetus becomes human at the moment of conception is a bad decision.

This approach does seem to meet Conditions 3 and 4, of the previous section. It seems, that is, to give us a basis for distinguishing good from bad decisions. A good decision is one that, in terms of its societal consequences, increases human happiness, while a bad decision is one that does not. Moreover, that basis does not permit us to distinguish one objectively correct decision from all others, since many decisions, incompatible with each other, may equally increase human happiness. We may then choose as we want among these satisfactory decisions. So Condition 3 is satisfied. Condition 4 also seems to be satisfied, because this basis for distinguishing good from bad decisions is justifiable (the increase in human happiness brought about by some decision is always a powerful argument for it), and it does appear to avoid the problem raised by the decisions of a prejudiced society (their decisions are bad ones since they lead to suffering for the minorities involved).

Further reflection reveals, however, that this approach is much less attractive than it seems at first sight. To begin with, it is in essence nothing but a straightforward utilitarianism that faces the standard objection[8] to utilitarianism: it fails to consider the question of justice. Even if a decision increases human happiness in general, it may nevertheless be an unjust decision, increasing general happiness only at the expense of the happiness of some minority.

This objection is especially important in our context, for we can see how it puts Glanville Williams's theory into a perspective that shows that it cannot really meet the problem of the decisions of a prejudiced society. After all, either he counts the happiness of only those making the decision or he counts the happiness of those being decided upon as well. If the former, then the prejudiced decision of a prejudiced society may be a good one, according to his criterion, since it may increase the happiness of the prejudiced majority at the cost (not to be counted) of the happiness of the minority the quality of whose humanity is being decided upon. If the latter, the prejudiced decision of a prejudiced society may still be a good one, on Glanville Williams's criterion, since it may still increase general happiness by increasing the happiness of the prejudiced majority sufficiently to outweigh the loss (which is counted) of the happiness of the minority the quality of whose humanity is being decided upon. Again, an unjust decision may be a good one according to his criterion.

Besides this problem, there remain the additional questions raised by Conditions 1 and 2, questions about which Glanville Williams's approach has nothing to say. Indeed, such questions may be compounded by his approach. After all, to him the humanity of the fetus depends upon the decisions as to its humanity made by that group of creatures whom we might call irreproachably human—the clear-cut humans—with the proviso that these decisions are to count only if they would, in light of their social consequences, increase the happiness of human beings. And Glanville Williams may mean just the happiness of these clear-cut human beings. His approach may therefore depend upon the notion of the clear-cut human beings at two stages: it is their decision that counts, and it counts if it has as a social consequence an increase in their happiness. The difficult problem of satisfying Conditions 1 and 2 is therefore doubly crucial for him.

All of this should, I believe, lead us to a growing suspicion about the soundness both of his specific approach and of the decisional approach in general.

4.4. Do Our Reactions Count?

All of the approaches we have considered so far have centered on the idea that the humanity of the fetus is determined by some conscious decision. But there is another, somewhat different, approach that we should consider. According to that approach, the humanity of the fetus is determined by the way in which we react to it. What counts are our attitudes and the ways in which we react and not our conscious decisions. But, like the decisional approach, this new approach makes the humanity of the fetus a function of the relations to it of some clear-cut human beings.

This position has been advanced most recently by Professor Wertheimer.[9] He claims that the defenders of fetal humanity draw their strength from noting the continuity of development at each stage from conception to full-fledged adulthood while the deniers of fetal humanity draw their strength from noticing the obvious differences between a fetus at conception and a full-fledged adult. Since there is, he concludes, much to be said for each side, the question arises as to how we are to resolve the dispute between them. The suggestion that Wertheimer is sympathetic to is that[10]

... what our natural response is to a thing, how we naturally react, cognitively, affectively, and behaviorally, is partly definitive of how we ought to respond to that thing. Often only an actual confrontation will tell us what we need to know, and sometimes we may each respond differently, and thus have different understandings.

It is this suggestion that we shall now consider.

Wertheimer himself is pessimistic about using his approach in the near future to resolve the problem of the status of the fetus. He feels that there would have to be serious modifications in the fetal condition before we could have enough interactions with and responses to the fetus so that we could discover what we feel about it. Moreover, whatever we might feel about this new type of communicating or observable creature is not clearly relevant to the status of fetuses as they now exist.

It is not clear that Wertheimer's pessimism is justified. Paul Ramsey[11] has called our attention to one possibility of studying human reactions to fetuses, even given their current state of existence, by letting people see pictures of them and their behavior and studying the responses that viewing such pictures elicit. Such an experiment has never been carried out, but there are at least some data that suggest that its results might be significant. When Lennart Nilsson's photographs of fetuses were published in *Life* in 1965, many readers wrote the magazine to report their reactions, which generally tended to be that they could no longer view the fetus, at least in the later stages of its development, as a disposable thing. Naturally, no conclusions should be drawn from this small sample, but it does suggest that, were we to adopt Wertheimer's approach, some progress could be made in arriving at a better consensus on the question of fetal humanity.

Of course, the question that we must consider first is whether we want to adopt this approach. The question is, once more, whether Wertheimer's suggestion satisfies Conditions 1 to 4. Like most other writers, he seems unaware of the problems that give rise to the need to satisfy Conditions 1 and 2; he deals only with the satisfaction of Conditions 3 and 4. He raises these issues by considering, as we did, the problem raised by the responses of a prejudiced society. He puts it as follows:[12]

We surely want to say that Negroes are and always have been full-fledged human beings, no matter what certain segments of mankind may have thought, and no matter how numerous or unanimous those segments were.

His problem is how to reconcile this realization with the view that the humanity of any entity is determined by how people respond to that entity.

It is obvious that Wertheimer can meet this problem only by ruling out certain responses, only by showing that certain responses are not relevant to the determination of the status of the creature in question. He offers us no full account of how he would do this, but we get some idea of what he has in mind as he attempts to establish the point that the response of the slaveholder to the Negro slave is irrelevant to the slave's true status: [13]

We argue that his form of life is, so to speak, an accident of history, explicable by reference to special socio-psychological circumstances, that are inessential to the nature of blacks and whites. The fact that Negroes can, and, special circumstances aside, naturally would be regarded and treated no differently than a Caucasian is at once a necessary and a sufficient condition for its being right to so regard and treat them.

Wertheimer seems to be suggesting the following theory: a decision to count an entity as a human being is a good one only if it is in accord with the natural responses of clear-cut human beings to the entity in question. This theory (a) is reasonable because it treats our natural responses as privileged, (b) solves the problem of the responses of the prejudiced society (for their responses are conditioned rather than natural), and (c) is not a criterion for the one objectively correct decision because conflicting responses to the same entity might satisfy this criterion. It may be, then, that we have a theory that at least satisfies Conditions 3 and 4.

I am not so sure. To begin with, can the distinction between the natural response and the sociopsychologically determined response do the work that Wertheimer needs it to do? I do not now want to raise

5 A Look at the Alternatives

The central question addressed in this chapter is when the fetus becomes a human being. We shall begin with a survey of the major alternatives that have been proposed and an analysis of their strengths and weaknesses. Our goal, however, is not merely to summarize possibilities; it is to show that the correct alternative only can be found on the basis of an adequate theory of essentialism and of the essential properties of human beings.

5.1. The Standard Alternatives

There are, naturally, a large number of possible positions that might be held on the issue of the point at which the fetus becomes a human being. But six alternatives seem to be most widely held: the moment of conception; the time (about the seventh or eighth day) at which segmentation, if it is to take place, takes place; the time (about the end of the sixth week) at which fetal brain activity commences; the moment (sometime between the thirteenth and twentieth week) of quickening, when the mother begins to feel the movements of the fetus; the time (about the twenty-fourth week) at which the fetus becomes viable, that is, has a reasonable chance of survival if born; and the moment of birth.

One way to understand these alternatives is to look at the major arguments offered for them by their adherents, beginning with the moment of conception:

1. At the moment of conception, the biological characteristics of the fetus have been determined by its genetic code. It is, from that point on, an individual unique creature, and everything that happens to it after that point is an unfolding of its unique selfhood. As Paul Ramsey[1] puts it:

Thus it might be said that in all essential respects the individual is whoever he is going to become from the moment of impregnation. He already is this while not knowing this or anything else. Thereafter, his subsequent development cannot be described as becoming some-the standard challenges to this distinction; rather, I should like to point out just how unclear the notion of the natural response is in this context. In one important sense, the slaveholder's response to the Negro is prefectly natural. Wertheimer himself says as much (without, I think, recognizing its full significance) in a footnote to his discussion of the slaveholder's response:[14]

> We develop our concept of a human through our relations with those near us and like us, and thus, at least initially, an isolated culture will generally perceive and describe foreigners as alien, strange, and not foursquare human.

On the other hand, there is an important sense in which an unprejudiced response is the natural one. As Huck Finn learned, when put into situations in which one lives with Negroes, one normal reaction is to respond to them as human beings. So, the viability of Wertheimer's solution to the problem raised by the reactions of the prejudiced society is very unclear, because, in this context, appeals to what is a natural response seem to lead to hopelessly conflicting results.

Second, it is not clear that this criterion is reasonable. Why should we ascribe to the natural response the special status implicit in Wertheimer's proposal? Why should we suppose that the natural response gives us any deeper insight into the status of the entity in question than some historically and/or sociopsychologically determined response? Indeed, implicit in Wertheimer's thesis may be a new, and far more dangerous, naturalistic fallacy, the fallacy of supposing that what is natural is somehow privileged.

I conclude, therefore, that this final attempt to save the decisional approach to the status of the fetus collapses. If so, then the suggestion is strong that we should abandon the decisional approach entirely and raise straightforwardly the question of when the fetus really does become a human being. By doing so, we shall of course be assuming that there is a single objectively correct account of the criterion for humanity, one that makes no reference to the decisions and attitudes of human beings. But in light of the analysis just completed, that assumption seems reasonable.

thing he is not now. It can only be described as a process of achieving, a process of becoming the one he already is. Genetics teaches us that we were from the beginning what we essentially still are in every cell and in every generally human attribute and in every individual attribute.

2. Until the moment of conception, the likelihood of the sperm and the ovum developing into a human being is very small. But once conception has taken place, the resulting fertilized cell has a very high probability of developing into a fully functioning human being. Indeed, four out of five of these entities are capable of surviving to birth. So the new entity, as opposed to the sperm and ovum, does have the right to life belonging to a human being. John T. Noonan, the leading advocate of this argument, says:[2]

... part of the business of a moralist is drawing lines. One evidence of the nonarbitrary character of the line drawn is the difference of probabilities on either side of it. If a spermatozoon is destroyed, one destroys a being which had a chance of far less than 1 in 200 million of developing into a reasoned being, possessed of the genetic code, a heart and other organs, and capable of pain. If a fetus is destroyed, one destroys a being already possessed of the genetic code, organs, and sensitivity to pain, and one which had an 80 percent chance of developing further into a baby outside the womb, who, in time, would reason.

3. There is a continuity of development from the moment of conception on. There are constant changes in the fetal condition, the fetus is constantly acquiring new structures and characteristics, but there is no one stage that is markedly different in quality from the previous or succeeding stages. Since that is so, there is no one stage in the process of fetal development that can plausibly be picked out as the moment at which the fetus becomes a human being. The moment of conception is, however, different in this respect. It marks the beginning of this continuous process of development and introduces something new that is radically discontinuous with what has come before it. Therefore, the moment of conception, and only it, is a plausible candidate for being that moment at which the fetus becomes a human being. Roger Wertheimer (who is not, himself, an advocate of this argument) summarizes this argument very well:[3]

. . . going back stage by stage from the infant to the zygote, one will
not find any differences between successive stages significant enough
to bear the enormous moral burden of allowing wholesale slaughter at
the earlier stage while categorically denying that permission at the
next stage.

In order to understand the second position, the position that the
fetus becomes a human being at that moment at which segmentation
(if it is to take place) takes place, it is necessary to remind ourselves
of one or two key points about early fetal development. When identical
twins develop from the fertilized ovum, a primitive streak across the
blastocyst signals the separation of the two entities. This occurs about
the seventh day after fertilization. Although it is nearly simultaneous
with implantation, it is an entirely separate process. And, of course,
it is a process peculiar to the development of identical twins. The
argument for treating the fetus as a human being from that point on
is very simple. The individual in question comes into existence as a
unique individual only at this point. Until then, there may be two
entities in the blastocyst. Paul Ramsey[4] was the first to raise this
argument (which we shall label Argument 4):

It might be asserted that it is at the time of segmentation, not earlier,
that life comes to be the individual human being it is thereafter to
be. . . . If there is a moment in the development of these nascent lives
of ours subsequent to fertilization and prior to birth (or graduation
from college) at which it would be reasonable to believe that an
individual human life begins and therefore begins to be inviolate, that
moment is arguably at the stage when segmentation may or may not
take place.

The next three positions to be considered (the moment at which
fetal brain activity begins, the moment of quickening, and the moment
of viability) share in common two basic beliefs: (a) the fetus does not
become human until it has far more of the abilities and structures of a
developed human being than it has at the moment of conception;
(b) there is some point between conception and birth at which the
fetus has acquired enough of these abilities and structures to be a

human being. These three positions differ only over the relevant abilities and structures.

The proponents of the claim that the fetus becomes a human being about six weeks after conception are primarily impressed with the fact that electroencephalographic waves are noticeable at that time,[5] and therefore the fetal brain must clearly be functioning. There are two main reasons for taking this development to be the one that marks the time at which the fetus becomes a human being:

5. The absence of electroencephalographic waves has come to be regarded by physicians as the indicator of the moment of death, the moment at which the entity in question is no longer a human being. So, on grounds of symmetry, it would seem appropriate to treat the appearance of such waves as the indicator of the moment at which the entity in question becomes a human being.[6] Callahan (who is not entirely convinced by this argument) puts it as follows:[7]

. . . it is very rare, for instance, to find a discussion of when life begins (pertinent to abortion) related to a discussion of when life ends (pertinent to euthanasia and the artificial prolongation of life). Yet both problems turn on what is meant by human life, and the illumination we gain in dealing with one of these problems will be useful when we deal with the other. Similarly, there is much to be said for trying to work out some consistent standards regarding the use of empirical data.

6. One of the characteristics essential to a human being is the capacity for conscious experience, at least at a primitive level. Before the sixth week, as far as we know, the fetus does not have this capacity. Thereafter, as the electroencephalographic evidence indicates, it does. Consequently, that is the time at which the fetus becomes a human being.

Those who claim that the fetus becomes a human being at the moment of quickening seem to be impressed by the following arguments:

7. Fetal movement is the most obvious sign of quickening. We would certainly want to think of the ability to move as one of those characteristics that are essential to human beings (not, of course, only to human beings). So it is at quickening, when there is a definite indication of

fetal movement, that we are justified in thinking of the fetus as a human being.

8. Only with quickening can the fetus be perceived by other human beings through ordinary means, for only then can the movement of the fetus be felt by the mother (and by others). Any entity that is not perceivable by other human beings cannot be a human being. So the fetus can become a human being only after the moment of quickening, only after the moment at which it enters into the realm of the perceivable.

The main argument for believing that the fetus becomes a human being at the moment of viability is the following:

9. How can anything be a human being if it is incapable of an independent existence? Only when the fetus becomes viable apart from its mother is it a human being.

The final position is that the fetus becomes a human being only at its birth. No special structure or capacity is developed at that point. Indeed, this is true of the fetus for the last few months of pregnancy. Those who argue for birth as the moment at which the fetus becomes a human being cannot therefore be doing so on the grounds that it is then that the fetus develops those structures and capacities that make it a human being. It is this absence of reference to developmental factors that sets this position off from the last three that we have considered. The main arguments for supposing that the fetus becomes a human being at the moment of birth seem to be these:

10. As long as the fetus is within the mother, it is more appropriately thought of as a part of the mother, rather than as a separate human being. That status is acquired by the fetus only when it emerges from the mother at the moment of birth.

11. While it is true that the fetus has the capacity for independent existence from the time of viability, it does not ordinarily enter upon that independent existence until birth. Previously, in its intake of oxygen and food, and its disposition of wastes, it is parasitic on the mother. Only at the moment of birth does the fetus acquire the independence essential to a human being.

12. It is only after birth that the fetus can interact with other humans. But such interaction, and not the mere abstract possibility of it, is an essential characteristic of a human being. So the fetus can be considered a human being only after birth.

We have before us, then, the six major definitions of the point at which the fetus becomes a human being and the principal reasons that are offered in their support. We are now in a position to begin evaluating them.

2. Tooley's Defense of Infanticide

Before turning to this evaluation, however, there is one point that should be noted. All of the positions that we are considering share the view that the fetus is a human being by the time that it is born. What they disagree about is whether and at what point the fetus acquires that status before birth. Consequently, all of these standard positions are consistent with our normal intuition that infanticide is morally objectionable.

In a recent much-discussed article,[8] Professor Michael Tooley challenges this basic assumption. Tooley claims that the infant at the moment of birth is not yet a "person" (Tooley's term for a human being with a serious right to life) and does not become one for some time after his birth. What leads Tooley to this unusual position? He reasons that the newborn child, as well as the fetus, fails to satisfy a necessary condition for being a person:[9]

An organism possesses a serious right to life only if it possesses the concept of a self as a continuing subject of experiences and other mental states, and believes that it is itself such a continuing entity.

Why does Tooley suppose that this condition must be satisfied by an organism if it is to be a person? He presents (pp. 46–47) the following argument:
1. To ascribe a right to an individual is to assert something about the *prima facie* obligations of other individuals to act, or refrain from acting, in certain ways.

2. But these obligations are conditional obligations.

3. In particular, "*a* has a right to *x*" should be analyzed as "if *a* desires *x,* then others are under a *prima facie* obligation to refrain from actions that would deprive him of it."

4. The right to life is the right to continue to exist as a subject of experiences and other mental states.

5. So "*a* has a right to life" should be analyzed as "if *a* desires to continue to exist as a subject of experiences and other mental states, then others are under a *prima facie* obligation not to prevent him from doing so."

6. But then *a* has a right to life only if *a* has a concept of a self as an enduring subject of experiences and believes that he is himself such an entity, for only then can *a* have the desire in question.

As far as I can see, the crucial steps in this argument are Steps 2 and 3. Why are the obligations in question conditional obligations and how does their being so lead to Step 3? Tooley offers the following brief argument at this crucial point:[10]

However, the obligations in question are conditional ones, being dependent upon the existence of certain desires of the individual to whom the right is ascribed. Thus if an individual asks one to destroy something to which he has a right, one does not violate his right to that thing if one proceeds to destroy it.

Professor Richard B. Brandt, in a passage referred to by Tooley, argues in a similar fashion for such an analysis:[11]

The final clause maintains that a right is an area of autonomy. Others are not obligated to perform for a person services that he does not want.

It seems to me that this argument is based upon a confusion. There is no doubt that a person can waive his rights; even if I have a right to *x,* you may deprive me of *x* if I ask you to (or even if I merely give you permission to). In that sense, rights are conditional. But Tooley goes on to conclude from that (in Step 3) that rights are conditional in a stronger sense, that I have actually to desire *x* in order for you

to be under a *prima facie* obligation to refrain from depriving me of it.
And this assertion certainly does not follow from Step 2 as defended
by Tooley.

There is another objection to Tooley's position. He himself recognizes that his analysis has to be modified:[12]

... in view of the above, an individual's right to *x* can be violated not
only when he desires *x*, but also when he would now desire *x* were it
not for one of the following: (1) he is in an emotionally unbalanced
state; (2) he is temporarily unconscious; (3) he has been conditioned
to desire the absence of *x*.

The point of this modification is to accommodate our intuitions that
there are cases in which an individual has a right to *x* even if he does
not desire that others forbear from depriving him of *x*. The obvious
question that Tooley's modification raises is why it should be restricted
only to these three cases? Why not add additional conditions that
would cover the newborn infant and even the fetus? Unless Professor
Tooley can justify his decision to specify three cases and no others,
he is open to the challenge that he has arbitrarily excluded the newborn
and the fetus from the class of persons.

We shall suppose therefore that Professor Tooley's position is
mistaken and return to the positions introduced in Section 5.1.

5.3. Some Preliminary Arguments

As one looks over the various arguments in Section 5.1, one is struck
by the fact that most of them are based upon a consideration of the
nature of fetal development and of the properties essential to human
beings. We shall be concerned with these arguments, and the theoretical
issues that they raise, for the rest of the book. But before doing so,
we must first examine the other group of arguments. I believe that we
can demonstrate that these arguments are defective and that, in fact,
the question of fetal humanity can only be settled by considering the
question of the essence of humanity.

Argument 1, the genetic argument, begins from the biological reality
that, at the moment of conception, the fertilized cell has the unique

chromosomal structure that will be found in all of the cells of the human being developing from that cell. But it goes on to conclude that the entity in question is already a human being. How does this conclusion follow from the premise in question? The mere fact that the fetus at the moment of conception shares a chromosomal structure with the fully developed human being hardly entails that the former is already a human being like the latter.

The idea behind the argument seems to be this: for any human being there is a set of properties that can properly be considered his basic attributes. Some of these are shared with other human beings while others are unique to the human being in question. Each human being has these properties owing to the chromosomal composition of his cells, and that chromosomal structure is therefore his ultimate property as a human being. The fetus already possesses that chromosomal composition at the moment of conception; so it is the same human being as the adult it later becomes.

This argument can also be put as follows: consider a human being A. He has certain basic properties, some of which he shares with other human beings and others of which he shares with no one. A and only A has got this complete set of properties. These properties are determined by the chromosomal structure of A, and that structure is his ultimate property beyond which no further reduction may be made. The fetus out of which A developed had that chromosomal structure from the moment of its conception. Therefore, that fetus is already identical with A and, like A, is a human being.

The first observation that should be made about this argument is that it assumes that all of the basic properties of a human being are genetically determined and that none is environmentally determined. It is, of course, difficult to decide whether or not this is so without an account of which properties are basic to individual human beings, but the justification for assuming that, whatever these basic characteristics are, they are all genetically determined is very unclear.

There is a further fallacy in the argument. Even if it is true that anything that possesses the basic properties of A is identical with A

and, like *A*, is a human being, and even if it is true that all of these
properties are determined by the chromosomal structure that the
fetus already has, it does not follow that the fetus already has all
of these properties. What the fetus has is the chromosomal mechanism
by which the properties are finally produced. Therefore, it does not
follow that the fetus out of which *A* will develop is identical with
A and, like *A*, is a human being. The argument from genetics will not
do.

We turn, therefore, to Argument 2, the argument from probabilities.
It is, from the very beginning, a difficult argument to follow. It
certainly does call attention to a difference between fetuses (even
from the moment of conception) on the one hand, and sperm and ova,
on the other hand. But it is not immediately clear how this difference
can be taken as evidence that the fetus (from the moment of conception) is a human being.

There is one passage in which Noonan explains the rationale for
this argument:[13]

I had supposed that the appeal to probabilities was the most common-
sensical of arguments, that to a greater or smaller degree all of us based
our actions on probabilities, and that in morals, as in law, prudence
and negligence were often measured by the account one had taken of
the probabilities. If the chance were 300,000,000 to 1 that the movement in the bushes into which you shot was a man's, I doubt if many
persons would hold you careless in shooting; but if the chances were
4 out of 5 that the movement was a human being's, few would acquit
you of blame in shooting.

To begin with, Noonan switches, at the key point at which he provides
us with his example, from the question of the morality of the action
to the very different question of the blameworthiness of the agent,
and the considerations that are relevant to the latter type of question
are not necessarily relevant to the former type of question. But more
important, the analogy is not very apt. In the case of the movement
in the bushes, the probability of four-fifths is the probability of the
entity in question's being human already. In the case of the fetus, the
probability of four-fifths is the probability of the entity in question,

without intervention, becoming a fully developed human being. Even
if we concede that we should suppose an entity is a human being
when the probability of its already being so is four-fifths, it does not
follow that we should suppose that an entity is a human being when the
probability of its becoming a fully developed human being is four-fifths.

There is, however, a different suggestion that may be advanced as
to the relevance of probability data. It is often claimed that the fetus
is a human being from the moment of conception because it has, from
that moment, the potential for engaging in typically human activities,
and it is the potential for doing that that distinguishes a human being.
But does the fetus really have this potential at the moment of conception? It may be argued that it does just because it has a four-fifths
probability of developing into a being that actually engages in these
activities. It should be noted, by the way, that the claim that the fetus
has these potentials can be reinforced by reference to the chromosomal
structure of the fetus which does provide a biological basis for these
potentials. But the important point is that the argument from probabilities, looked at this way, has become an argument about the essence
of humanity, just like the other arguments that we still have to consider.
After all, looked at this way, Noonan's claim is that the fetus is a
human being because it has a certain potential, and having that potential is what is essential to a human being.

This argument raises serious questions. It may be claimed, in objection
to the idea that at the moment of conception the fetus has the potential essential to a human being because it has the biological basis for
that potential, that something more is required if the fetus is truly
to be said to possess such potential. After all, consider as an example
a typical human activity, thinking. Human beings can think only if
they possess certain neural structures. Would not it be reasonable to
say that an entity has the potential of engaging in that activity only
when these structures are present?[14] And if so, we certainly cannot
say of the fetus, at the moment of conception, that it has the potential
of engaging in thought. A similar argument could, of course, be raised

in connection with other typically human activities.

The defender of the argument from probability might reply in this way: there are many different senses of "potential," and it is only in some senses of that term (the ones connected with the probability of later engaging in these activities) that the fetus, from the moment of conception, has the potential for engaging in typically human activities. But all that is required for being human is the possession of the potentiality of engaging in typically human activities in the weaker statistical sense. So the fetus is a human being from the moment of conception.

But this response is inconclusive because it offers no defense of its claim that the possession of the weaker statistical type of potentiality is all that is required for being a human being. Moreover, it never considers the possibility that actually engaging in some human activity, in addition to the potential (in any sense) of doing so, is required if the entity in question is to be human. There is, after all, a certain intuitive plausibility to the latter claim. If we suppose that a sufficient condition for being human is regularly engaging in typically human activities, then is not it plausible to suppose (admittedly, it does not follow) that the potentiality of engaging in these activities is sufficient only for being a potential human being? It is increasingly clear that Noonan's statistical considerations, no matter how interpreted, do not entail that the fetus is a human being from the moment of conception.

We turn now to Argument 4, the argument that the fetus becomes a human being at the moment of segmentation:

a. Until the time of segmentation, but not thereafter, it is physically possible that more than one human being will develop out of that which resulted from the fertilization of the ovum by the sperm.

b. Therefore, that which results from the fertilization of the ovum by the sperm (i) cannot be a human being until the time of segmentation and (ii) is a human being after that time.

It is unclear how either part of b follows from a. Why should (i) be true just because a is true? The following suggests itself: if the

fetus were a human being at some time before segmentation and then
were to split into two human beings, then we would have one human
being becoming two, and that is not possible. Unfortunately, although
initially persuasive, this argument must be rejected. One amoeba can
become two, so why cannot one human being become two?[15]

It is equally unclear why it should be thought that (ii) should follow
from a. Even if we suppose that (i) follows, this means only that the
fetus, by the time of segmentation, has passed one hurdle in becoming
a human being. The fetus is now a unique individual that will not split
into two others. But it certainly does not follow that all the hurdles
have been passed, it certainly does not follow that the fetus is a human
being after the time of segmentation.

Actually, as one examines the context in which Ramsey offered this
argument, one sees that something like this happened: Ramsey believed
(mistakenly, as we have seen) that the arguments from genetics and
probabilities show that the fetus is a human being from the moment of
conception. But he also believed (also mistakenly, as we have seen)
that (i) follows from a. So he concluded that (ii) is true. While we can
see how Ramsey was led to conclude that (ii) is true, (ii) is not justified,
and we can reject Argument 4.

We come finally to the very weak Argument 10, the argument that
claims that the fetus is not a human being until the moment of birth
because, until then, it is within the mother and ought to be thought of
as part of her. The inference here seems to be from the fetus's (A's)
being in the mother (B) to its being a part of the mother and not an
independent entity. But one certainly cannot infer from the fact that
A is within B that A is a part of B (and certainly not that A is not an
independent entity). I am in this room, but I am certainly not a part
of this room. Jonah in the whale was certainly not a part of the whale.
To be sure, the fetus is also dependent upon the mother. That is, of
course, a very different matter, and Argument 11, which raises it, is
a serious argument that cannot be dismissed so easily. For the moment,
we need note only that the mere fact that the fetus is in the mother
says nothing about its status as a human being.

5.4. The Matter of Essentialism

As generally presented, all of the remaining arguments, with one
exception, take the following form: there is a certain property essential
to being a human, and no human being does not have it; this property
is acquired by the fetus at a certain time; therefore, the fetus becomes
a human being at that time. Naturally, all of these arguments stand or
fall on their claims as to the property that is essential and as to when
it is acquired. They therefore raise the question as to how we are to
determine whether a given property is essential to an object of a given
type.

Actually, the same question is also raised by the one remaining
argument that does not have the foregoing form, the argument from
continuity, 3. According to that argument, there is no one stage in
fetal development that is radically different in quality from the preceding or succeeding stage. Now how are we to interpret this claim?
It may simply mean that the fetus is not, at any given instant of time,
radically different from what it was the instant before or after, but on
that interpretation it would show only that becoming a human being is
not an instantaneous process; it would certainly not entail the conclusion of the argument, namely, that there is no one moment in the
course of fetal development after which the fetus is so radically
different from what it was at earlier stages as plausibly to uphold the
claim that the fetus was not a human being then but is now. If the
argument from continuity is to have any weight, we must suppose
that the claim of the continuity of fetal development instead means
that there is no property acquired by the fetus after conception that
is essential to being human, and the argument concludes that the fetus
must therefore be human from the moment of conception. But if this
is the point of departure for Argument 3, then it also raises the question
of how we are to determine whether a given property is essential to
a given type of object.

In order to deal properly with the difficult problem of what properties are essential for being human, it will be necessary for us to articu-
late and defend a full theory of essentialism. But before we do so,

there is one general point about the arguments that we are considering that should be noted now.

None of the arguments, as they are usually presented, is formally valid. After all, they all have the following structure:

There is a property P which is such that every human being must have it (it is essential for being human); when the fetus acquires that property P, it becomes a human being.

Unless, as does not seem reasonable, humanity can be shown to depend on one property alone, such an argument is invalid. If, for example, there are two such properties, P and Q, the mere possession of one cannot make the fetus a human being as long as it does not possess the other. So the desired conclusion does not follow from the premise.

If the arguments we are considering are to be taken seriously, they must be reformulated as follows:

There is a property P which is such that every human being must have it (it is essential for being human); by the time an entity acquires P, it has every other property Q that is such that every human being must have Q; when the fetus acquires property P, it becomes a human being.

Even with this reformulation, however, the argument is still not valid. All that the premises guarantee is that, when the fetus acquires P, it will have satisfied all the necessary conditions for being human, it will have all the properties that human beings must have. It does not follow from that that the fetus has satisfied any specific condition that is sufficient for being human. To be sure, we could validly infer that the fetus is not a human being before it acquires P, but that is not what we want. We want to know when it does become a human being.

This objection is a serious one, but we shall see in Chapter 7 that it can be met in light of the theory of essentialism that we will present. We turn then to a general consideration of essential properties, with a recognition that the arguments about fetal humanity that do not consider the question of the essence of humanity have been shown to be in error.

6 A Theory of Essentialism

The question that we are concerned with is when the possession of
a given property is essential (necessary) for membership in a given class.
However, I want to put that question aside for now, for reasons that
will emerge shortly, to consider the related question of when a given
object has a property essentially (necessarily). These are different
questions, since one has to do with the conditions under which an
object is a member of a given class, while the other has to do with the
conditions under which a given object must have a given property.
But an answer to the latter question helps provide an answer to the
former one.

  This discussion is, of necessity, a metaphysical discussion, and there
are, no doubt, many who would prefer that the question of fetal
humanity be settled without considering metaphysical questions. But
we concluded in Chapter 5 that the standard attempts to do so are
unsatisfactory and that all of the remaining arguments and positions
concerning fetal humanity raise these metaphysical issues. Moreover,
with the collapse of logical positivism and its verifiability theory of
meaning, we need no longer be hesitant about entering into responsible
metaphysical investigations.

  In the first section of this chapter, I will set out in an intuitive fashion
a theory of essentialism. (A formal presentation of the theory, together
with an explanation of the ways in which it differs from the current
alternative theories, occurs in the Appendix. The formal presentation
is technical, and the reader who is not familiar with the current
literature may well wish to ignore it.) In the second section, I shall use
my theory of the essential properties of objects to construct a theory
of when the possession of a given property is essential for membership
in a given class.

6.1. An Introduction to Essentialism
What is the distinction between the properties that an object has essentially and the properties that an object has accidentally? It is the

following: on the one hand, there are some properties that an obejct must have; if the object did not have them, it would not exist at all. These are the properties that an object has essentially. On the other hand, there are some properties that an object has but might not have. The possession of these properties are not necessary for the object's existence. These are the properties that an object has accidentally.

There are two obvious questions that are raised by this distinction: (a) What does it mean to say that an object must have a property, as opposed merely to saying that it has the property but might not? (b) How can we tell which properties are possessed by an object essentially and which are possessed by an object accidentally? It is important to keep in mind that these are two different (although obviously related) questions. One is concerned with the meaning of certain claims, the other with how we come to know whether these claims are true or false. And it may be the case (although I think that it is not) that we know what these claims mean without knowing how to tell whether they are true or false.

Many philosophers believe that these questions cannot be answered and therefore reject all talk about essential properties. Some scholars are not so sure and in recent years have attempted to develop answers to these questions (especially the first, crucial one). Many such attempts are based on the Leibnizian idea of a logically possible, but not actual, situation (this is usually called a logically possible or, simply, a possible world). The assertion is that an object has a property essentially and necessarily just in case it has that property, not merely in the actual world, but in all possible worlds, or, at least, in all possible worlds in which the object exists. On the other hand, the argument continues, an object has a property accidentally just in case it has that property in the actual world but there are possible worlds in which it does not have the property.

Even this attempt is, however, not entirely satisfactory. After all, what does it mean to say that some object a has the property P in some possible world? Presumably it means that there is some object b in that possible world that is identical with *a* and has *P*. But what does it mean to say that *b* is identical with *a*? In short, what does identity across possible worlds mean? If (as many philosophers believe) that question cannot be answered, then appealing to the idea that an object has a property in all possible worlds does not shed much light upon the idea that an object has a property necessarily.

Perhaps an example will help make this point clearer. Consider the big tree on my front lawn. Is it necessarily a tree? Could it have been something else? Well, we can easily imagine a possible world in which there is a big rock on my front lawn but no tree. Is that a world in which my tree is a rock? That depends on whether the big thing on my lawn in that possible world is identical with my tree in the actual world. Given that we have no understanding of this cross-world identity, the very meaning of that question (and also any possible answers to it) is very unclear.

For these reasons, I have proposed an alternative approach to essential properties. According to this alternative approach, an object has a property necessarily (and essentially) if it cannot lose it without going out of existence. On the other hand, it has the property accidentally if it can change and lose that property without going out of existence. Thus, for example, it is an accidental property of my tree that it has 832 leaves on it. After all, it can grow an additional leaf or one can fall off and the tree will continue to exist. On the other hand, if it were chopped down and cut into lumber, so that there was no tree there anymore, my tree would have gone out of existence. The property of being a tree is, in my account, essential to the tree on my lawn.

Let us put this definition a little more carefully. If, before a change, there was an object *o* with a property *P,* then the change is what we can call an alteration (as against a substantial change) if *o* continues to exist after the change though it no longer possesses *P*. On the other hand, the change is a substantial change if, after its occurrence, *o* no longer exists. Then we shall say that an object *o* has a property *P* accidentally just in case it has P and its loss of P would be an alteration, but it has P essentially just in case it has P and its loss of P would be a substantial change.

This is the theory of essentialism that we will be working with for the rest of the book. It is developed, as I noted, in a fuller but more technical fashion in the Appendix.

6.2. Natural Kinds and Essential Properties

We return now to our original question of how to determine what properties are essential (necessary) for membership in a given class. In order to deal with it, however, one final concept must be introduced. We shall say that any property had essentially by some object and accidentally by none (whether actual or potential) determines what is called a natural kind and that the set of objects having that property is a natural kind. In short, a natural kind is a set of objects each of which has a certain property necessarily (with the proviso that nothing else has that property). The set of trees is one example of a natural kind, since each tree necessarily has the property of being a tree (it would go out of existence if it stopped being a tree) and nothing but trees are trees. But the set of white objects is not a natural kind, since not every white object has the property of being white necessarily. Many (perhaps even all) could have their color changed while still continuing to exist.

I should now like to introduce several claims about what properties are essential for membership in a natural kind:

1. Only the possession of properties had essentially by every member of a natural kind is necessary (essential) for membership in that natural kind.

2. The possession of all properties had essentially by every member of a natural kind is sufficient for membership in that natural kind.

Claim 1 tells us which properties are such that their possession is essential (necessary) for membership in natural kinds, while Claim 2 tells us which properties are such that their concurrent possession is sufficient for membership in natural kinds.

Both of these claims would be false if they were extended to classes in general. Consider the class of white objects. While being white is not a property had essentially by every member of that class, it is necessary (essential) for membership in that class. So Claim 1 would be false if it were extended to cover nonnatural kinds. Similarly, it seems that the only properties had essentially by every member of this class are those had essentially by all colored objects, but the possession of these properties is not sufficient for membership in the class of white objects. What is sufficient is being white. So Claim 2 would also be false if it were extended to cover nonnatural kinds.

Intuitively, what is happening here is the following: assume that there are, for each class, some properties such that the possession of each of them is necessary and their concurrent possession is sufficient for membership in the class in question. Now 1 claims that the only necessary properties are those had essentially by all members of that class, and 2 claims that their concurrent possession is a sufficient condition for membership in that class. These conclusions must be false in the case of nonnatural kinds, for there are no properties that their members, and only their members, have essentially and the possession of which could be the necessary and sufficient conditions for membership in the class in question. But in the case of a natural kind, where there are properties that all members have essentially and nothing else has at all, it is plausible to conjecture that the possession of these properties is necessary and sufficient for membership in the natural kind. This is, of course, precisely what is claimed in 1 and 2.

I have no proof that 1 and 2 are true. But they are intuitively plausible and no counterexamples seem to be forthcoming. So I will tentatively adopt them and use them when we consider, in the next chapter, the question of the essence of humanity.

7 The Essence of Humanity

In this chapter, we shall use the results of our discussion in Chapter 6 to determine what properties are essential for being human; in light of that exposition, we shall try to determine that point at which the fetus becomes a human being.

7.1. Humanity as a Natural Kind

An important step in this process is to decide whether or not the class of human beings is a natural kind. Obviously, all and only the members of the class of human beings have the property of being human. If, then, every member of that class has that property essentially, if no human being can stop being a human being and still exist, then the class of human beings will be a natural kind.

Consider the moment of death. It would be wrong to think of it just as a moment at which the human being undergoes a significant alteration. Rather, it is the moment at which he stops being human and goes out of existence. This is why death is so different from anything else that happens to us. We survive those other occurrences, however they may change us, but we do not survive our deaths. As Wittgenstein[1] put it: "Death is not an event in life: we do not live to experience death." So a human being goes out of existence when he stops being human, being human is therefore an essential property of every human being, and humanity is a natural kind.

It is probably obvious to note that, in saying that a human being goes out of existence when he dies (but not when he loses his memory or experiences a severe change of character, for example), I am not also saying that no part of him continues to exist. His body exists for some time after death, and in some views what is called the soul does as well. But the human being has gone out of existence.[2]

The following objection might be raised: it is true that, in the normal course of events, when a human being is no longer a human being, it also no longer exists. But perhaps there are ways in which human beings could stop being human beings but still continue to exist. Consider the

respiratory activity. Doctors would test for such cessation by using
ors to detect emission of breath and seeking the pulse to detect
inued circulation. It was recognized that death could be brought
by the destruction of other systems and organs (the liver, the
, the brain), but it was generally thought that their destruction
about death by affecting the functioning of heart and lung.
roach is summarized in the following definition of death:[6]

ation of life; the ceasing to exist; defined by physicians as a
page of the circulation of blood, and a cessation of the animal
functions consequent thereon, such as respiration, pulsation,

ition has, of course, come under important challenge in
. There is a growing tendency to define death in terms of
cessation of brain function. It is increasingly felt that
essation, rather than a cessation of cardiac and respiratory
essence of death.
e in the development of this revisionist approach is
eport of an Ad Hoc Committee of the Harvard Medical
eared in the *Journal of the American Medical Associa-*
hat report clearly suggests a movement away from the
ch to death and toward the "brain-death" approach
pular one; we should note, in using it, that it con-
hetorical lode). The authors suggest a variety of
ermining brain death. These include tests for
nsitivity, for spontaneous movement, and for
also suggest that a flat (or isoelectric) EEG could
death.[8]
rticularly be noted about their recommendations.
at a flat EEG can be taken as definitive of death.
a way of confirming the presence of an irre-
good reasons for treating flat EEG's as only
ome well-documented cases, a flat EEG
everal hours and was followed by complete

---

case of Gregor in Kafka's *Metamorphosis*. Has not he survived his
amazing transformation although he is no longer a human being? And
given that this is so, it follows that being human is not an essential
property of human beings.

It is very difficult to know what to say about this objection because
it is very difficult to know what to say about the case of Gregor.
Despite its literary strength, it is not clear that Kafka has succeeded in
presenting us with a coherent picture of Gregor in an insect's body.
But assume that he has. The objector seems to be impressed with the
continuities through this change when he assures us that it still is
Gregor and with the discontinuities when he assures us that it is no
longer a human being. The justification for this asymmetrical treatment
is unclear. To the extent that one thinks that it is still Gregor, should
not one also think that it is a human being (even if in the body of a
bug), and to the extent that one thinks that it is not a human being,
should not one think that it is not Gregor (even if it does have many
of his thoughts, feeling, and emotions)?

Moreover, there is an important methodological point to note here.
We have throughout this book emphasized the use of self-evident
intuitions as a source of knowledge, and we have tried to elicit intuitions about many unusual cases. But these have all been quite closely
tied to reality. Those who raise the case of Gregor, however, turn to
the fictional and break sharply with reality, and it is just at this point,
it seems to me, that a reliance on intuitions is most debatable.

We may, then, keeping in mind our Claims 1 and 2 of the previous
chapter with regard to the properties that are necessary and sufficient
for membership in a natural kind, proceed with our evaluation of the
remaining arguments from Chapter 5. Their common structure (slightly
restated from Section 5.4) was the following:

a. There is a property P that is such that its possession is essential for
being human;

b. By the time an entity acquires P, it has every other property Q that
is essential for being human;

c. When the fetus acquires P, it becomes a human being.

There were two major problems with each of these arguments: how to tell whether their essentialist claims are true, and how to modify them so that the appropriate step of Type c will follow from the appropriate steps of Types a and b. We now see how to solve these problems. Since humanity is a natural kind, the only properties essential for being a human being, given our Assumption 1, are those had essentially by every human being, are those such that their loss would mean that the human being in question would go out of existence. We can therefore use the going-out-of-existence text to determine the truth of the claims of Types a and b in any given argument. And given our Assumption 2, the claim of Type c does follow straightforwardly from the claims of Types a and b.

In short, then, our technical excursus has put us in a position to deal with the problem of the essence of humanity. What we must first see is what properties are such that their loss would mean the going out of existence (the death) of a human being. We turn therefore to an analysis of death.

7.2. The Analysis of Death

The question of when a human being is dead has become one of great importance in recent years. Two factors are primarily responsible. The first is the growing frequency of transplants of vital organs. From the point of view of the recipient of the transplant, it is at the present state of medical science preferable that the organ be removed from the donor's body as soon as possible (organ banks are a conjecturable development for the future). However, there is a strong moral feeling[3] that, no matter how definitely incurable is the illness of the donor and no matter how close to death he may be, it is wrong to remove the organ until the point of natural death has passed. It is therefore extremely important to develop a precise definition of the moment of death so as to satisfy both of these demands (as much as may be possible) by taking the organ from the donor's body as soon as possible after that point.

The second factor influencing our preoccupation with this definition

is the growing technological ability to maintain vit? artificial means when they no longer operate natu that we ought to continue to do so after the per there is some feeling that, no matter how incur his illness to be and how close to death he is, supply this artificial maintenance so long as becomes extremely important to know wh

Because it is these two factors that hav emphasis on the issue of defining death two extremely significant cautionary r Professor David Daube:[4]

The question of at what moment i' nary or even ordinary measures to ' fused with the question of at wha of such measures is often justif?

Even if Daube's last claim is t would be permissible, and p medical measures intended not yet dead. The relief o such cases. Consequent' when a person dies an measures, these are r important cautiona

If no person's de use in a transpla not for this pu man has died

Again, whe the purpo a definit? more s? settle?

Tra?

recovery. The coma was due in those cases to severe barbiturate poisoning, and in such cases, as well as in cases of hypothermia (in which the body temperature may fall below 90°F), flat EEG readings are not even good indicators of an irreversible coma.

What arguments are offered by the Ad Hoc Committee for its recommendations? They emerge best in its criticism of the traditional definition of death:[9]

From ancient times down to the recent past it was clear that, when the respiration and heart stopped, the brain would die in a few minutes; so the obvious criterion of no heart beat as synonymous with death was sufficiently accurate. In those times the heart was considered to be the central organ of the body; it is not surprising that its failure marked the onset of death. This is no longer valid when modern resuscitative and supportive measures are used. These improved activities can now restore "life" as judged by the ancient standards of persistent respiration and continuing heart beat. This can be the case even when there is not the remotest possibility of an individual recovering consciousness following massive brain damage. In other situations "life" can be maintained only by means of an artificial respiration and electrical stimulation of the heart beat.

This passage deserves careful attention since it contains the core of the argument for redefining death. Unfortunately, it is poorly argued, since there are three rather different arguments suggested in it. The first is suggested by the opening passages: There are cases in which the patient's brain has not died but in which the heart and respiratory system have stopped and will not revive naturally. In such cases, the heart and respiratory system can be revived artificially and will, after a period of time, function naturally and spontaneously. According to the classical definition, the patient has died but has been medically resurrected. It would seem more reasonable to abandon this definition and replace it with one that avoids the element of resurrection. We should therefore adopt the brain-death definition and treat the person as dead only when his brain has died. The second argument is suggested by the closing passages of the quotation: there are cases in which the patient suffers massive brain damage and is clearly dead though his respiration and circulation can be kept functioning by artificial means. According to the traditional definition, such a patient is still alive. Therefore, the traditional definition should be rejected in favor of a definition that treats someone as dead when the brain has died.

The second of these arguments is clearly in error. Proponents of the traditional definition, one may reasonably conclude, were talking about spontaneous cardiac and respiratory functions and not artificially supported functions. They were not, therefore, necessarily committed to the view that the patients referred to in the second argument ought to be regarded as still alive. The first argument is not open to this objection, but it can be met by modifying the classical definition so that it refers to an irreparable cessation of spontaneous and natural cardiac and respiratory functions. Then the first objection is not valid, for it deals with cases in which spontaneous and natural cardiac and respiratory functions can be revived. According to our revised version of the classical definition, the patient has not died, for those functions have ceased only temporarily and, after interim support, will resume naturally.

All of this leads us, however, to still a third argument suggested by the quotation:
1. There are cases in which a person's heart beats spontaneously even though his brain is in irreversible coma.
2. In such cases, even according to the classical definition of death as we have revised it, the person is alive.
3. But he clearly is dead.
4. Therefore, we should revise the definition so that death is the cessation of brain function.
This last argument brings us to the crux of the issue—is Step 3 true? Paul Ramsey,[10] for one, thinks that it is not:

It is one thing to declare a person to be obviously still alive so long as he has an indefinitely fully functioning brain in the absence of heart or lung function. It would be quite another thing to declare a person dead (because his brain is past full recovery) in the presence of a still continuing, natural functioning of lungs and/or heart.

These are, I find, very puzzling differentiations. One can easily understand, with Ramsey, that as long as the brain still functions naturally, the absence of spontaneous circulation and respiration does not indicate death (we have had no trouble regarding people in iron lungs or using pacemakers as alive). The traditional definition of death, we could all agree, needs to be modified one more time to read: a person is dead only if there has been an irreparable cessation of spontaneous and natural cardiac and respiratory functions and there has been an irreparable cessation of brain function. But suppose we have the latter condition without the former one, the brain has ceased to function but the heart and lungs have not. Ramsey is correct in calling attention to this case as different from its reverse. Is the person dead if his brain has suffered irreparable and massive damage whatever the state of the heart and lungs?

As we use the concept of death to help us determine what is essential for being human, we will remember that there remain some fundamental questions to which we are unable to make precise answers. This is not surprising in light of the complexity of human life. We shall try to reduce this difficulty by continuing our argument in ways compatible with both definitions of death, traditional (as modified in light of our discussion of it) and revisionist.

7.3. The Essence of Humanity

We shall first consider the question of what properties are essential to being human if we suppose that death and the passing out of existence occur only if there has been an irreparable cessation of brain function (keeping in mind that that condition itself, as we have noted, is a matter of medical judgment). We shall then consider the same question on the supposition that Ramsey's more complicated theory of death (the modified traditional view) is correct.

According to what is called the brain-death theory, as long as there has not been an irreparable cessation of brain function, the person in question continues to exist no matter what else has happened to him. If so, it seems to follow that there is only one property—leaving aside those entailed by this one property—had essentially by each human being (and therefore that there is only one property which is essential to humanity), namely, the possession of a brain that has not suffered an irreparable cessation of function.[11]

Several consequences follow immediately from this conclusion. Returning to Arguments 5 to 9 and 11 to 12 of Chapter 5, we can see that, with the exception of Arguments 5 and 6, which refer to the functioning brain, all are unsound because all contain some essentialist claim we now know to be false. Argument 7 claims that movement, or perhaps just the ability to move, is essential for being human. That claim is false. A human being who has stopped moving, and even one who has lost the ability to move, has not therefore stopped existing. Being able to move, then, and, a fortiori, moving are not essential properties of human beings and are not therefore essential to being human. Argument 8 claims that being perceivable by other human beings is essential for being human. But that is also false. A human being who has stopped being perceivable by other humans (one isolated, for example, on the other side of the moon, out of reach even of radio communication) has not therefore stopped existing. Being perceivable by other human beings is not an essential property of human beings and is not therefore essential to being human. And the same point can be made about the claim in Argument 9 that viability is essential for being human, the claim in Argument 11 that independent existence is essential for being human, and the claim in Argument 12 that actual interaction with other human beings is essential for being human. The loss of none of those properties would mean that the human being in question had gone out of existence, so none of them can be essential to that human being and none of them can be essential for being human.

Let us now look at Arguments 5 and 6, modified by the general point we made at the end of Chapter 5 and amalgamated into one argument:

The property of having a functioning brain (or, at least, a brain that, if not functioning, is susceptible of function) is one that every human being must have because it is essential for its being human; by the time that an entity acquires that property, it has all the other properties that are essential for being human; the class of human beings is a natural kind; therefore, when the fetus acquires that property, it becomes a human being.

It is clear that the property in question is, according to the brain-death theory, one that is had essentially by all human beings. The question that we have to consider is whether the second premise ("by the time . . . essential for being human") is true. It might appear that its truth does follow from the brain-death theory. After all, we did see earlier that that theory entails that only one property (together with those entailed by it) is essential for being human. Nevertheless, rather than relying solely on our earlier argument, we shall adopt an alternative approach to strengthen the conviction that this second premise is true. What we shall do is note the important ways in which the fetus resembles, and differs from, an ordinary human being by the time it definitely has a functioning brain (about the end of the sixth week of development). It shall then be fairly evident, in light of our theory essentialism, that none of these differences involves the lack of some property in the fetus that is essential for its being human.

Structurally, there are few features of the human being that are not fully present by the end of the sixth week. Not only are the familiar external features and all the internal organs present, but the contours of the body are nicely rounded. More importantly, the body is functioning. Not only is the brain functioning but the heart is beating sturdily (the fetus by this time has its own completely developed vascular system), the stomach is producing digestive juices, the liver is manufacturing blood cells, the kidney is extracting uric acid from the blood, and the nerves and muscles are operating in concert so that reflex reactions can begin.

What are the properties that a fetus acquires after the sixth week of its development? Certain structures do appear later. These include the fingernails (which appear in the third month), the completed vocal cords (which also appear then), taste buds and salivary glands (again, in the third month), and hair and eyelashes (in the fifth month). In addition, certain functions begin later than the sixth week. The fetus begins to urinate (in the third month), to move spontaneously (in the third month), to respond to external stimuli (at least in the fifth month), and to breathe (in the sixth month). Moreover, there is a constant growth in size. And finally, at the time of birth, the fetus ceases to receive its oxygen and food through the placenta and starts receiving them through the mouth and nose.

We shall not examine each of these properties (structures and functions) to show that they are not essential for being human. The procedure is essentially the one we used earlier to show that the essentialist presuppositions of 7 through 9 and 11 to 12 are in error. We might therefore conclude, on the supposition that the brain-death theory is correct, that the fetus becomes a human being about the end of the sixth week after its development.

There is, however, one complication that should be noted here. There are, after all, progressive stages in the physical development and in the functioning of the brain. For example, the fetal brain (and nervous system) does not develop sufficiently to support spontaneous motion until some time in the third month after conception. There is, of course, no doubt that that stage of development is sufficient for the fetus to be human. No one would be likely to maintain that a spontaneously moving human being has died, and similarly, a spontaneously moving fetus would seem to have become human. One might, however, want to claim that the fetus does not become a human being until the point of spontaneous movement. So, then, on the supposition that the brain-death theory of death is correct, one ought to conclude that the fetus becomes a human being at some time between the sixth and twelfth week after its conception.

What if we reject the brain-death theory, however, and replace it with its equally plausible contender, Ramsey's theory of death? According to that theory, which we can call the brain, heart, and lung theory of death, the human being does not die, does not go out of existence, until such time as the brain, heart, and lungs have irreparably ceased functioning naturally. What are the essential features of being human according to this theory?

Actually, the adoption of Ramsey's theory causes no major modifications. According to that theory, what is essential to being human, what each human being must retain if he is to continue to exist, is the possession of a functioning (actually or potentially) heart, lung, or brain. It is only when a human being possesses none of these that he dies and goes out of existence. And the fetus comes into humanity, so to speak, when he acquires one of these.

On Ramsey's theory, the argument would now run as follows:

The property of having a functioning brain, heart, or lungs (or at least organs of the kind that, if not functioning, are susceptible of function) is one that every human being must have because it is essential for being human; by the time that an entity acquires that property, it has all the other properties that are essential for being human; the class of human beings is a natural kind; therefore, when the fetus acquires that property, it becomes a human being.

There remains, once more, the problem of the second step ("by the time . . . essential for being human"). Since the fetal heart starts operating rather early, it is not clear that Step 2 is correct. Many systems are not yet operating, and many structures are not yet present. Still, following our theory of essentialism, we should conclude that the fetus becomes a human being when it acquires a functioning heart (the first of the organs to function in the fetus).

There is, however, a further complication here, and it is analogous to the one encountered if we adopt the brain-death theory: When may we properly say that the fetal heart begins to function? At two weeks, when occasional contractions of the primitive fetal heart are present? In the fourth to fifth week, when the heart, although incomplete, is beating regularly, pumping blood cells through a closed vascular system, and the tracings obtained by an ECG exhibit the classical elements of an adult tracing? Or after the end of the seventh week, when the fetal heart is functionally complete and "normal"?

In short, then, we have not reached a precise conclusion in our study of the question of when the fetus becomes a human being. We do know that it does so sometime between the end of the second week and the end of the third month. But it surely is not a human being at the moment of conception, and it surely is one by the end of the third month. Though we have not come to a final answer to our question, we have narrowed the range of acceptable answers quite considerably.

7.4. In Response to Callahan

It is clear that the position that we have been advocating in this chapter places us among the members of the developmental school (as this term is used by Daniel Callahan)[12] and certainly shows our agreement with those who believe that the fetus becomes a human being at some stage in development. Indeed, the position that we are advocating was first suggested to us by a reading of Callahan's account of that school. But Callahan rejects the whole approach of the school, and it behooves us to consider why.

Callahan's first objection is that[13]

If one chooses to use a development criterion, there are any number of stages other than that of brain development that might be chosen. Implantation, gastrulation, the presence of all organs, completion of the brain structure, "quickening," viability, birth and so on have each been suggested as the dividing line by different commentators in recent history. Why choose one rather than another?

Essentially, we ourselves raised this problem in Chapter 5, and the whole purpose os these last two chapters has been to meet this challenge by defending the reasonableness of a particular dividing line. If our argument has been successful, we need not worry about this objection of Callahan's.

The second more serious objection has to do with the matter of potentials. Callahan introduces it with the following remark:[14]

Yet it (the developmental approach) is not without its difficulties. One of these is that it does not give wide range to the concept of "potentiality." A zygote has, genetically (dependent upon successful development), the potentiality to become a "person."

But we have already seen in Chapter 5 that the mere possession of that potential does not make the fetus a human being. Callahan, however, goes on to make the following very suggestive remark:[15]

An objection to the use of a common criterion of life for both nascent embryos and dying persons might be based upon one important distinction. In the case of an irreversible coma (signalled by a flat EEG), it is not the coma as such but the irreversibility which is the critical condition. For with the "death" of the brain . . . comes the loss of all potentiality for personhood. . . . In the instance of a zygote or early embryo, however, even before the advent of brain waves—the potentiality for personhood exists.

This passage suggests, from our perspective, the following argument: the moment at which the human being goes out of existence occurs at that point at which the potential for continued performance of certain functions is no longer present. Brain death (or brain, heart, and lung death) is considered the moment of death because it is then that potential ceases. But if that is so, then the property that an entity must have in order to be a human being, the property that is essential for humanity, is the possession of that potential. The fetus has that from the moment of conception, and since nothing else is essential for being human, the fetus is a human being from the moment of conception. We can therefore view Callahan as attempting to revive, by appeal to our own criterion of essentialism, the argument of potential that we rejected in Chapter 5.

It seems to me that this point is ultimately in error. In order to see why, let us imagine the following science-fiction case:[16] imagine that medical technology has reached the stage at which, when brain death occurs, the brain is removed, "liquefied," and "recast" into a new functioning brain. The new brain bears no relation to the old one (it has none of its memory traces, and so on). If the new brain were put back into the old body, would the same human being exist or a new human being who made use of the body of the old one? I am inclined to suppose the latter. But consider the entity whose brain has died. Is not he like the fetus? Both have the potential for developing into an entity with a functioning brain (we shall call this a weak potential) but neither now has the structure of a functioning brain. We can conclude, it seems to me, that an entity can go out of existence even if it retains a weak potential for having a functioning brain, and that, analogously, the fetus is not a human being just because it has this weak potential. What is essential for being human is the possession of the potential for human activities that comes with having the structures required for a functioning brain. It is this potential that the fetus acquires at (or perhaps slightly before) the time that its brain starts functioning, and it is this potential that the newly conceived fetus does not have. Once and for all, then, we can lay this matter of potential to rest.

Part III

8 Some Further Questions

Our rather laborious consideration seems to have led us to the following result: at some point between two and twelve weeks after conception, the fetus becomes a human being with all the rights to life (to use that phrase) belonging to such an entity. Thereafter—with the exception of one special case—it is wrong for the mother to abort the fetus, even if her life is threatened by its continued existence. Moreover, there should be strict laws against abortion, although there may be good reasons for not treating abortions as ordinary homicides.

We have not yet dealt with several additional issues about abortion, and I should like to raise two of them in this chapter. One of these questions concerns the status of the fetus, and the morality of abortion, before the fetus becomes a human being. The other concerns the obligations of society to those women who do not abort their fetuses and to their resulting children.

8.1. The Status of Abortions before Fetal Humanity

Is the question of the morality of abortion in the first few weeks after conception of any practical importance? After all, in the vast majority of cases, by the time there is certainty of pregnancy, and by the time that practical arrangements for abortion can be made, the fetus is already a human being (particularly if we suppose that the fetus is human by the end of the eighth week).[1] It may be argued, then, that there is no point to discussing the morality of abortions in the first few weeks after conception.

I think that this view is mistaken for several reasons. To begin with, there is a variety of contraceptive devices and therapies (either in use or development) that function by preventing the implantation of the fetus in the uterine wall. These include the intrauterine device (or I.U.D.) and some of the proposed morning-after pills (so-called). It is important to understand that such methods are not merely contraceptive, that they produce abortions at a very early stage of fetal development. If so, the moral permissibility of their use presupposes the moral permissibility of abortion in the first few weeks after conception. Second, there has been much recent discussion of the technique of "menstrual extraction," which is employed on the person whose menstrual period is late without a medical determination of pregnancy. If pregnancy exists, an abortion is induced by this technique. If it does not, the menstruation is induced. The principal value of this technique is that it enables the individual to obtain an abortion, if she is pregnant, without the time lapse required by a formal determination. This technique, as well, would not be morally permissible if there were moral objections to the performance of abortions in the first few weeks after conception. Finally, there are cases (rape is the most important of these) in which, if there are no moral objections to early abortion, it is appropriate to use the technique of menstrual extraction to prevent forced pregnancy.

If the arguments we have considered are correct, then abortion performed in the first few weeks after conception is not the taking of the life of a human being. It does not follow, however, that early abortion is morally permissible, because there may be other moral objections to it. We turn to these.

What are the arguments that can be advanced against early abortion? The following come to mind:

a. Abortion, a certain group has alleged, allows women—and men—to avoid the consequences of what I suppose may still be called sexual license and therefore encourages promiscuity. There should be laws against abortion, then, even if performed before the fetus becomes a human being.

b. The prohibition of abortion, even when the fetus is still only a (weakly) potential human being, is a way of society to express and confirm its view of the absolute inviolability of human life; on the other hand, permission of abortion, even at this early stage, tends to compromise this sense of the value of human life.

c. Even if the fetus is not a human being (as we have defined that entity)

at this early stage, it is still a (weakly) potential human being with
rights. Abortion is therefore objectionable because it violates the
rights of this potential human being.
d. And if the fetus is not a human being at this early stage, it is a
living creature with some rights. Abortion is therefore objectionable
because it violates such rights.

There are several important differences between arguments a and
b, on the one hand, and Arguments c and d, on the other. The former
arguments are really directed against a social policy of allowing abortions in the early stages of fetal development. Their burden seems to
be that such a social policy would subvert the foundations of our
morality—would, as is often said, "weaken the moral fabric of society."
The latter two arguments are directed against the intrinsic morality
of early abortion. They claim that such abortions violate the rights
of the fetus. They grant, to be sure, that at this stage the fetus is not
yet a human being, but they claim that it nevertheless has some rights
that are violated by the act of abortion.

It is relatively easy to evaluate arguments a and b. Their claims about
the social consequences of abortion are suspect. There is no evidence
that persons (male and female) have ever been discouraged from
engaging in sexual activities because they knew that there were laws
against abortion. Further, there may well be no social interest in limit-
ing sexual activity. One person's promiscuity is another person's sexual
freedom, and one may turn Argument a on its head and argue that we
should allow abortions, at least at these early stages, so as to promote
the sexual liberation of society. And is there really any reason to
suppose that the permissibility of abortion, especially if it is limited
to the early stage, has in any way reduced or impaired the sense of
inviolatibility that surrounds human life? Moreover, the proponents
of Arguments a and b fail to take into account the many social benefits
of allowing abortion at the early stage, social benefits that may well
outweigh any of the problems such abortions may raise. In short, these
arguments on the ground of social consequences are weak.

It is far more difficult to evaluate Arguments c and d because they raise two very difficult questions: (1) Does the fetus, at these early stages, have the claimed right to life, and (2) are there any interests of the mother that outweigh this right to life?

It is important to understand why these questions are so difficult to answer. They raise, in effect, the problem of whether any entities other than human beings have a right to life, and, if so, what the strength of the rights of those entities may be. It would seem that such problems can be approached only by considering the very basis of the right to life and existence, in the broadest of contexts, including, possibly, all organisms and objects. The resolution of Questions 1 and 2 raises such fundamental moral questions as clearly to exceed the compass of the current inquiry.

It may be helpful to think of the difficulty this way: in dealing with abortion after the fetus has become a human being, we argued by use of example and analogy. Principles enabling us to make determinations in the question of abortion were proposed on the ground that they offered intuitively acceptable results in analogous cases or criticized on the ground that they failed to do so in such analogous cases. The whole method worked only because we were able to discover a large number of analogous cases about which we had clear intuitions. But, as we come to deal with Questions 1 and 2, that simple method fails us, and it is not clear what method of reasoning we are to employ in its stead. The question of the moral permissibility of abortions at the earliest stage of fetal development must therefore be left unresolved unless some other appropriate method of argument is found, and the search for such a method is bound to be a complex one.

8.2. The Responsibility of Society

Let us suppose that the policies advocated in this book were adopted and that, in particular, there were strict laws against abortion (at least after the third month following conception). Let us suppose, moreover, that some women did not obtain abortions after that time, either because abortion was illegal and the laws prohibiting it were effectively enforced or because they recognized the immorality of obtaining

abortion. Obviously, certain social problems would result. The life
or health (mental or physical) of some women would be threatened
by the continuation of pregnancy. For some families, the new child
would constitute a great burden, economically, psychologically, or in
other ways. The mode of existence and careers of some women would
be seriously disrupted. Physically or mentally damaged infants would
be born. Each of these circumstances has penalties that must be
understood in human as well as abstract sociological terms. I give them
quick summary here, but the reader must, as I think I do, feel a keen
empathy for the persons affected by them.

Means exist of alleviating most (but perhaps not all) of these problems. Adequate medical care could preserve the lives and restore the
health of those endangered or impaired by continuation of pregnancy
to term. The burden created by the children born as a result could
be relieved by financial assistance, family therapy, and day-care
services, among other kinds of support. The question arises whether
the provision of such aid constitutes an obligation upon all.

This question, I note, is about a uniform obligation, and not about
the kind of weaker responsibility that is denoted for most of us by
the idea of charity, in which we are not morally compelled to provide
aid, though our doing so may be morally meritorious. The demand
of charity normally make a less rigorous and certainly less universal
claim than the claim that society has an obligation to relieve the
burden I have described, and I am concerned now with the truth of
the stronger claim.

This last point is worth considering more carefully because it has
implications for a great many other issues. Our society already makes
some effort to aid those in need—the poor, the very young, the very
old, the impaired and the imperiled. Is this aid an act of charity—assistance provided without moral imperative—or does society have an
obligation to supply it? The argument is sometimes made that no
extension of this effort should be contemplated because the resulting
demand upon society would be disproportionately large. The strength
of such an argument surely depends upon whether providing aid of

the kind is an obligation or an act of charity. If the former, then the peril of the demand, so to speak, has to be comparable to the peril of the need before society is excepted from its obligations. But if the latter, then a far weaker peril may be considered sufficient for exception. The same point can be made in the specific case of the need created by the avoidance of abortion. If society is under the clear obligation to meet that need, then only the most pressing circumstances would be sufficient to void that obligation.

Are we under that specific obligation? Two circumstances in the avoidance of abortion seem to give rise to such an obligation: (a) that the need for aid arises from the doing of what is right and (b) that society has mandated the avoidance of abortion by prohibiting it by law. Let us look more closely at both.

One might argue as follows: the need for aid could have been prevented by abortion. Abortion was not obtained, and that is the cause of the need. A person who is in need because he is done what is right is a person whom society is under an obligation to aid.

The trouble with this argument is that it rests upon an unacceptable general principle. Does society have an obligation, for example, to aid anyone who is in need and who could have removed or prevented that need by killing another? Any such person experiences need because he has done what is right. There are perhaps certain types of heroic behavior of such a nature that society is under an obligation to aid those who are in need because of performing those heroic acts. Refraining from committing murder is, however, not such a heroic act. It is a requirement of morality that we must all fulfill, and we have no claim against society merely because we are in need owing to our having fulfilled this requirement. The trouble with the argument that we are considering is that it fails to take into account the nature of abortion.

A similar point can be raised against the following argument: when society passes laws against abortions and enforces them, it is compelling the bearing of children and all the consequences that result from it. By doing so, society incurs the obligation to compensate the human beings affected by that compulsion by bearing the cost of their burdens (to the extent that that is possible, and it must always be remembered that there are certain burdens that allow no means of compensation).

There is no doubt that when society infringes upon individual rights in a way that results in a loss to the people concerned, society must compensate those people for the loss. But the women in question had no right to abort their fetuses, and society, in passing laws against abortion, in no way infringed upon their rights. Why, therefore, does society have any obligation to aid them?

In short, then, the view that society has an obligation specially to aid women who do not have abortions, their families and their children, is substantially weakened by the consideration that abortion, after the earliest stage of pregnancy, is an act of murder.

We have implicitly asserted, in differentiating between the motives of charity and the mandates of obligation, that we are not bound to come to the aid of any other individual on the basis of need alone. It is still possible to claim, however, that in our corporate existence as a society, we have serious public policy reasons for aiding these women. After all, if past experience is any guide, women in trouble will be tempted by the illegal abortionist and many will procure illegal abortions. One way to minimize the number of such abortions is to aid, in such ways as possible, those who choose to bear their child. We have therefore strong reasons, in our corporate existence as a society, to provide the aid that we have been discussing, at least until we reach the point at which the peril of the demand begins to approach the peril of the need.

9 Abortion and the Supreme Court

On January 22, 1973, the Supreme Court announced its decision in two cases challenging existing abortion laws. These decisions have, at least for the time being, settled many fundamental aspects of the legal status of abortion in the United States. The decisions of the Court are in profound contrast to the position that we have advocated in this book. We shall therefore devote this penultimate chapter to a consideration of the Court's arguments.

9.1. The Decision in *Roe* v. *Wade*

Two decisions were announced by the Court on January 22. The first (*Roe* v. *Wade*) involved a challenge to a Texas law prohibiting all abortions not necessary to save the life of the mother. The second (*Doe* v. *Bolton*) tested a Georgia law incorporating many of the recommendations of the Model Penal Code as to the circumstances under which abortion should be allowed (in the case of rape and of a defective fetus, as well as when the pregnancy threatens the life or health of the mother), together with provisions regulating the place where abortions can be performed, the number of doctors that must concur, and other factors.

Of these two decisions, the more fundamental was *Roe* v. *Wade*. It was in this case that the Court came to grips with the central legal issue, namely, the extent to which it is legitimate for the state to prohibit or regulate abortion. In *Doe* v. *Bolton,* the Court was more concerned with subsidiary issues involving the legitimacy of particular types of regulations.

The Court summarized its decision in *Roe* v. *Wade* as follows:[1]

(a) For the stage prior to approximately the end of the first trimester/three months/the abortion decision and its effectuation must be left to the medical judgment of the pregnant woman's attending physician.
(b) For the stage subsequent to approximately the end of the first trimester, the state, in promoting its interest in the health of the

mother, may, if it chooses, regulate the abortion procedure in ways that are reasonably related to maternal health.

(c) For the stage subsequent to viability, the state, in promoting its interest in the potentiality of human life, may, if it chooses, regulate, and even proscribe, abortion except where it is necessary, in appropriate medical judgment, for the preservation of the life or health of the mother.

In short, the Court ruled that abortion can be prohibited only after viability and then only if the life or health of the mother is not threatened. Before viability, abortions cannot be prohibited, but they can be regulated after the first trimester if the regulations are reasonably related to maternal health. This last clause is taken very seriously by the Court. In *Doe* v. *Bolton,* instances of regulation in the Georgia code were found unconstitutional on the ground that they were not reasonably related to maternal health.

How did the Court arrive at this decision? In Sections V and VII of the decision, it set out the claims on both sides. Jane Roe's argument was summarized in these words:[2]

The principal thrust of appellant's attack on the Texas statutes is that they improperly invade a right, said to be possessed by the pregnant woman, to choose to terminate her pregnancy.

On the other hand, the Court saw as possible legitimate interests of the state the regulation of abortion, like other medical procedures, so as to ensure maximum safety for the patient and the protection of prenatal life. At this point in the decision, the Court added the following very significant remark:[3]

Logically, of course, a legitimate state interest in this area need not stand or fall on acceptance of the belief that life begins at conception or at some other point prior to live birth. In assessing the state's interest, recognition may be given to the less rigid claim that as long as at least potential life is involved, the state may assert interests beyond the protection of the pregnant woman alone.

In Sections VIII to X, the Court stated its conclusion. It viewed this case as one presenting a conflict of interests, and it saw itself

as weighing these interests. It began by agreeing that the woman's
right to privacy did encompass her right to decide whether or not to
terminate her pregnancy. But it argued that this right is not absolute,
since the state's interests must also be considered:[4]

We therefore conclude that the right of personal privacy includes the
abortion decision, but that this right is not unqualified and must be
considered against important state interests in regulation.

The Court had no hesitation in ruling that the woman's right can be
limited after the first trimester because of the state's interest in preserving and protecting maternal health. But the Court was less prepared
to agree that the woman's right can be limited because of the state's
interest in protecting prenatal life. Indeed, the Court rejected Texas's
strong claim that life begins at conception, and that the state therefore
has a right to protect such life by prohibiting abortion. The first reason
advanced for rejecting that claim was phrased in this way:[5]

We need not resolve the difficult question of when life begins. When
those trained in the respective disciplines of medicine, philosophy,
and theology are unable to arrive at any consensus, the judiciary, at
this point in the development of man's knowledge, is not in a position
to speculate as to the answer.

Its second reason was that[6]

In areas other than criminal abortion, the law has been reluctant to
endorse any theory that life, as we recognize it, begins before live
birth or to accord legal rights to the unborn except in narrowly defined
situations and except when the rights are contingent upon live birth.

The Court accepted the weaker claim that the state has an interest in
protecting the potential of life. But when does that interest become
compelling enough to enable the state to prohibit abortion? The
Court said:[7]

. . . the compelling point is at viability. This is so because the fetus
then has the capacity of meaningful life outside the mother's womb.
State regulation protective of fetal life after viability thus has both
logical and biological justifications. If the state is interested in pro-

tecting fetal life after viability, it may go so far as to prescribe abortion during that period except where it is necessary to preserve the life or health of the mother.

9.2. The Court on Potential Life

I want to begin by considering that part of the Court's decision that allows Texas to proscribe abortions after viability so as to protect its interest in potential life. I note that it is difficult to evaluate that important part of the decision because the Court had little to say in defense of it other than the paragraph just quoted.

There are three very dubious elements of this ruling:
1. Why is the state prohibited from proscribing abortions when the life or health of the mother is threatened? Perhaps the following argument may be offered in the case of threat to maternal life: the mother is actually alive but the fetus is only potentially alive, and the protection of actual life takes precedence over the protection of potential life. Even if we grant this argument, why is the state prevented from prohibiting abortion when only maternal health is threatened? What is the argument against the claim that protecting potential life takes precedence in that case?
2. Why does the interest in potential life become compelling only when the stage of viability is reached? The Court's whole argument for this claim is[8]

This is so because the fetus then presumably has the capacity of meaningful life outside the mother's womb.

There is, no doubt, an important type of potential for life, the capacity of meaningful life outside the mother's womb, that the fetus acquires only at the time of viability. But there are other types of potential for life that it acquires earlier. At conception, for example, the fertilized cell has the potential for life in the sense that it will, in the normal course of events, develop into a human being. A six-week-old fetus has the potential for life in the stronger sense that all of the major organs it needs for life are already functioning. Why then does the state's interest in protecting potential life become compelling only at the point of viability? The Court failed to answer that question.

3. It can fairly be said that those trained in the respective disciplines of medicine, philosophy, and theology are unlikely to be able to arrive at any consensus on the question of when the fetus becomes potentially alive and when the state's interest in protecting this potential life becomes compelling enough to outweigh the rights of the mother. Why then did not the court conclude, as it did when it considered the question of fetal humanity, that the judiciary cannot rule on such a question?

In pursuit of this last point, we approach the Court's more fundamental arguments against prohibiting abortion before viability.

9.3. The Court on Actual Life

The crucial claim in the Court's decision is that laws prohibiting abortion cannot be justified on the ground that the state has an interest in protecting the life of the fetus who is a human being. The Court offered two reasons for this claim: that the law has never yet accorded the fetus this status, and that the matter of fetal humanity is not one about which it is appropriate for the courts to speculate.

The first of the Court's reasons is not particularly strong. Whatever force we want to ascribe to precedent in the law, the Court has in the past modified its previous decisions in light of newer information and insights. In a matter as important as the conflict between the fetus's right to life and the rights of the mother, it would have seemed particularly necessary to deal with the issues rather than relying upon precedent.

In its second argument, the Court did deal with those issues by adopting the following principle:

1. It is inappropriate for the Court to speculate about the answer to questions about which relevant professional specialists cannot arrive at a consensus. This principle seems irrelevant. The issue before the Court was whether the Texas legislature could make a determination

in light of the best available evidence and legislate on the basis of it. Justice White, in his dissent, raised this point:[9]

The upshot is that the people and legislatures of the fifty states are constitutionally disentitled to weigh the relative importance of the continued existence and development of the fetus on the one hand against the spectrum of possible impacts on the mother on the other hand.

This objection could be met, however, if we modified the Court's principle in the following way:

2. It is inappropriate for a legislature to write law upon the basis of its best belief when the relevant professional specialists cannot agree that that belief is correct.

On the basis of such a principle, the Court could argue that Texas had no right to protect by law the right of the fetus to life, thereby acknowledging it to be a human being with such a right, because the relevant specialists do not agree that the fetus has that right. As it stands, however, Principle 2 is questionable. In a large number of areas, legislatures regularly do (and must) act upon issues upon which there is a wide diversity of opinion among professional specialists. So Principle 2 has to be modified to deal with only certain cases, and the obvious suggestion is

3. It is inappropriate for the legislature, on the ground of belief, to write law in such a way as to violate the basic rights of some individuals, when professional specialists do not agree that that belief is correct.

This principle could be used to defend the Court's decision. But is there any reason to accept it as true? Two arguments for this principle immediately suggest themselves: (a) If the relevant professional specialists do not agree, then there cannot be any proof that the answer in question is the correct one. But a legislature should not infringe the rights of people on the basis of unproved belief. (b) When the professional specialists do not agree, there must be legitimate and reasonable alternatives of belief, and we ought to respect the rights of believers in each of these alternatives to act on their own judgments.

We have already discussed in Chapter 3 the principles that lie behind these arguments. We saw there that neither of these arguments, as applied to abortion, is acceptable if the fetus is a human being. To employ these arguments correctly, the Court must presuppose that the fetus is not a human being. And that, of course, it cannot do, since the aim of its logic is the view that courts and legislatures, at least at this juncture, should remain neutral on the issue of fetal humanity.

There is a second point that should be noted about Principles 1 to 3. There are cases in which, by failing to deal with an issue, an implicit, inevitable decision is in fact reached. We have before us such a case. The Court was considering Texas's claim that it had the right to prohibit abortion in order to protect the fetus. The Court conceded that if the fetus had a protectable right to life, Texas could prohibit abortions. But when the Court concluded that it (and, by implication, Texas) could not decide whether the fetus is a human being with the right to life, Texas was compelled to act as if the fetus had no such right that Texas could protect. Why should Principles like 1 to 3 be accepted if the result is the effective endorsement of one disputed claim over another?[10]

There is an alternative to the Court's approach. It is that each of the legislatures should consider the vexing problems surrounding abortions, weigh all of the relevant factors, and write law on the basis of its conclusions. The legislature would, undoubtedly have to consider the question of fetal humanity, but, I submit, the Court is wrong in supposing that there is a way in which that question can be avoided.

9.4. Further Considerations

There is one final set of issues raised by the Court's opinion that should be considered. In an interesting footnote,[11] the Court argued that Texas's law is inconsistent with Texas's announced goal of protecting the fetus's right to life because (a) it makes an exception when the mother's life is threatened, (b) it punishes the abortionist and not the mother, and (c) it provides a lesser penalty than the penalty prescribed for murder. This argument seems to me questionable.

As we learned in Chapter 3, someone committed to the view that abortion is murder is not necessarily committed to the view that the laws prohibiting the murder by abortion should be identical to those prohibiting murder by other means. Indeed, the law already differentiates among varieties of murder in other areas. There might well be public-policy or human considerations favoring separate, different laws of prohibition of abortion. While I would not necessarily defend all of the provisions of the Texas law, I think that we can identify and appreciate the considerations that might lead to the formulation of such a law.

Two of the provisions the Court specifically notes seem in fact to be reasonable. The woman who obtains an abortion is often operating under extreme stress and is not an appropriate subject of the force of the law. One might well decide to provide only for the punishment of the abortionist. Second, one might well decide that in light of the current public uncertainty about the morality of abortion, the abortionist should receive a lesser penalty than that received by other murderers. One might admit that the guilt of the abortionist may be extenuated by the uncertainty in his mind about the morality of abortion.

I do not want to defend the provision allowing abortion when the mother's life is threatened. We saw in Chapter 1 that the fact that the pregnancy threatens the life of the mother does not usually justify abortion. But I think we can understand why Texas included that exception in its laws. The legislature may well have been under the misapprehension that abortions are permissible in such cases as acts of self-defense.

In short, then, the Court's charge of inconsistency is unsupported. More important, it is not the case that those who believe in fetal humanity are committed to laws prohibiting abortion that are identical to laws prohibiting murder.

9.5. Conclusion

The Supreme Court has ruled, and the principal legal issues in this country are, at least for now, resolved. I have tried to show, however, that the Court's ruling was in error, that it failed to grapple with the crucial issues surrounding the laws prohibiting abortion. The serious public debate about abortion must, and certainly will, continue. I hope this book will contribute to that debate.

10 Epilogue

Abortion remains an important issue, though I am aware that there is a group of scholars and lay people who regard further discussion of it as fruitless or even eccentric. They are as certain of the resolutions they have made as I myself was when I was first asked to deal with the subject. It is easy enough to take the fetus, hidden and unknown, as a being alien from humanity and to give no more thought to its destruction than to drowning of an unwanted kitten. Or, I suppose more correctly, even less thought, for I am aware that those who argue for unrestricted abortion have their own humane convictions, and many of them probably could not bring themselves to kill an animal but would support its life, make room for it, assume the burden of its dependence.

How can this be? Three answers come to mind. The first is that the killing of the fetus seems to be a necessary expedient to human, and particularly feminist, libertarianism. The second is that the killing of the fetus is done by a medical procedure, and the same science that ordinarily preserves life in this case terminates it, and in such an abstract and "sanitary" manner that the real nature of the act can be quite suppressed. The third is that pressing world problems of over-population and malnutrition can be used to provide a kind of social certification of the rightness of the act.

We are by this time familiar enough with the method of argument by intuition and analogy used in this book, I hope, to be able to discover for ourselves that all of these answers are flawed. These flaws are not only errors but dangers to us and to all human kind. It is not necessary to prove that the world is now facing a variety of critical problems; the evidence is all around us. It is necessary, however, to point out strongly that in the kinds of remedies adopted, particularly to those problems that touch human life, we may either confirm and fulfill the moral intuitions that perhaps may be the ultimately distinguishing characteristic of humanity or abandon them and, believing we are safeguarding the species, actually set ourselves in the path that

er of convention whether a given o_1
nge, this seems to be a mistake. Is it, for
ntion whether we continue to exist after
haven't we insured our immortality a long
it seems obviously true that trees stop
urnt down, but not when they lose a branch,
long time before there were people who had
dentity of trees. So our distinction cannot be
s. To be sure, there are undoubtedly many
e to decide whether what has occurred is an
ntial change, and this has perhaps led some people
whole distinction is merely a matter of convention.
weak argument; it could, after all, be applied
ctions about which there are borderline cases, viz.,
The existence of decisions merely indicates that
he cases, not that the distinction is based upon

ometimes supposed that whether a given change is an
ubstantial change depends upon how we classify the
when we refer to it. Thus, if I describe my red desk
it by use of 'my red desk', thereby classifying it as a
en a change in its color would constitute a substantial
uld not, however, if I merely classify it as a desk by
it by use of 'my desk'. This supposition also seems to be
begin with, it is open to all of the types of objections
nst the view that the distinction is conventional. Moreover,
s to be nothing wrong with saying 'my red desk could
be painted green without its stopping to exist because it is
green.' There is nothing wrong with saying this because
eferring here, both when one uses 'my red desk' and when
s 'it', to the same substance, one that can persist through
s in its color. So red desks, even when referred to in such a way
olves their color, can lose that color and still continue to exist,
he supposition we are considering is straightforwardly false.

can lead only to loss of that characteristic and, in a much more profound sense, to the destruction of what it is we are trying to preserve.

Already the global planners who seek to limit growth are using the word "triage"—a technical term applied to the treatment of battlefield casualties on the basis of a priority established by chance for survival—to describe the tasks ahead of us. Is there famine? Let some starve. Is there overpopulation? Correct it by famine. Do the old and the defective need help to survive? Do not supply it.

We make a mistake if we think this is a new issue. To "decrease the surplus population" is a phrase we all remember, and it contains a motive that is as old as humanity itself. War is nothing but the implementation of that motive by public policy.

Surely the urgent needs I describe require response. But they require a response that is consistent with our moral values. We can, of course, free ourselves from those values, but it is a stunted, faltering freedom that is the result. Surely, moreover, as we develop more accurate definitions of our needs, we ought to raise new solutions. But if the character of humanity is to survive, these solutions must be founded in our moral history. The great task before us is to find a better understanding of that history and to make a better application of it.

I cannot imagine a moral argument that is not ultimately founded in intuition. Whatever we do, we act with what we have, and there is no way of getting beyond it. I suppose that is what the psalmist had in mind when he sang, "It is He Who has made us, and not we ourselves." And how we use intuition is to work by analogy, by moving from those circumstances in which our intuition is sure to connected circumstances that are the objects of our inquiry.

The opportunities for the application of this method, are, of course, immense.

Appendix
A Formal Theory of Essentialism

I should like in this appendix to explain and defend the theory of essentialism that I set out in Chapter 6 and elsewhere.[1] In particular, I should like to show that (a) it is based upon a simple distinction that we can often employ without any difficulty, (b) it is open to none of the standard objections to essentialism, and (c) it recognizes as essential significant properties of particular physical objects, most importantly, the ones that correspond to the intuitively appropriate Aristotelian secondary substances. If all of this can be done, then there will be no reason to offer, as recent defenders of essentialism like David Kaplan and Alvin Plantinga have, some de dicto reinterpretation of essentialist claims. This is fortunate, for the theory in question does not seem to lend itself to such reinterpretations. In short, then, I will be arguing for an unabashed traditional theory of Aristotelian essentialism.

A.1. Essentialism Based upon the Theory of Change

On my account, all essentialist claims are based upon a distinction between types of changes first drawn by Aristotle, a distinction between alterations, on the one hand, and comings-to-be and passings-away (which we shall refer to from now on as substantial changes), on the other hand. He[2] set out that distinction as follows:

Since, then, we must distinguish (a) the substratum and (b) the property whose nature it is to be predicated of the substratum; and since change of each of these occurs; there is alteration when the substratum is perceptible and persists, but changed in its own properties, the properties in question being opposed to one another either as contraries or as intermediaries . . . But when nothing perceptible persists in its identity as a substratum, and the thing changes as a whole . . . such an occurence is no longer alteration. It is a coming-to-be of the one substance and a passing-away of the other. . . . If, however, in such cases, any property persists in the thing that has come-to-be the same way as it was in the thing which has passed-away, . . . the second thing, into which the first changes, must not be a property of this persistent identical something. Otherwise, the change will be alteration.

(4) This distinction is applicable to changes involving both concrete and abstract objects. In the case of abstract objects, however, something very strange happens. While one can imagine[5] alterations involving abstract objects—four used to be my favorite number, but it isn't any more—it seems impossible for there to be a substantial change involving one. This is due to the fact—at least, to what we all assume, for reasons that are unclear, is a fact—that abstract objects exist necessarily and cannot go out of existence as they would if they were involved in substantial changes.

(5) This distinction is one that we are all quite familiar with and can use, quite comfortably, in many cases in which questions of identity and continued existence are of importance. One notable example of its use occurs when we think about human death. What makes us treat it so differently from other changes involving human beings is precisely that it, but not the other changes, is the going-out-of-existence-of, and not merely an alteration in, the person in question. This distinction is also used, of course, in more prosaic cases. If your car is insured, then lots of things can happen to your car, and it will still be insured (unless, of course, the insurance is formally cancelled). It can be painted, you can change the engine, etc. But if it is entirely flattened and made into sheet metal from which a car is made, then your insurance would not cover the new car since the new car is not identical with your old covered car. The changes that the old car underwent, unlike the paint job and the engine job, were substantial changes and not mere alterations.

Given this distinction, we are now in a position to introduce a very simple theory of essentialism. We shall say that an object o_1 has a property P_1 essentially just in case o_1 has P_1 and would go out of existence if it lost it: just in case the loss of it would involve a substantial change. We shall say that an object o_1 has a property P_1 accidentally just in case o_1 has P_1 but could lose it without going out of existence: just in case the loss of it would involve a mere alteration.

In light of what we have seen so far about our distinction between alterations and substantial changes, we can immediately say the follow-

ing about the distinction between essential and accidental properties:
it is a distinction that applies equally to concrete and abstract objects;
it is based upon neither our conventions nor our way of classifying
objects; and it is one that we can often operate with without any
difficulty, although there will certainly be many borderline cases in
which we will have to decide whether a property is essential or accidental.

It is important to note that it does not follow from the above definition of 'essentially' that if o_1 has a property P_1 essentially, then there
is some name n_1 which either necessarily names o_1 or is a proper name
of o_1 and which is such that $\ulcorner P_1 n_1 \urcorner$ necessarily expresses a truth. Since
the existence of such a name is required for any of the presently
suggested de dicto reinterpretations of essentialist claims,[6] it must be
admitted that they cannot be used to interpret our claims to those
who only admit de dicto modal claims. But, I submit, if our program
is successful, there will be no reason to be disturbed by this lack of
a de dicto reinterpretation.

A.2. Solving the Problems of Essentialism
Three standard objections have been raised against essentialism, one
having to do with referential opacity, one having to do with the
different classes to which objects belong, and one having to do with
the problem of identity through possible worlds. It is now well known
that the first two of these objections are based upon a confusion, so
I will just briefly explain what is wrong with them and spend most of
my time on the third problem, the one which has not yet been dealt
with satisfactorily and which our theory of essentialism solves very
neatly.

As far as referential opacity is concerned, the objection runs as
follows: consider the claims that

(1) Nine is essentially greater than seven
and

(2) The number that I am thinking about now is essentially greater than seven,

and suppose that I am now thinking about nine. Then, these claims should both be true or both be false since they both say of the same object that it has the same property essentially. But, so the argument goes, (1) is true and (2) is false. After all, I could have been thinking about five, and then the number that I would be thinking about now would be less than seven. So there is something wrong with essentialist claims, and they should be rejected. The answer to this objection is very simple: (2) is true, just as (1) is, for the number that I am thinking about now could not be altered so as to be less than seven. The reason why one thinks that (2) is false is that I could have been thinking about some other number which is less than seven, but all that that shows is that the very different claim that

(2′) 'The number that I am thinking about now is greater than seven' is necessarily true

is false. As long as you do not reinterpret (2) so that it means (2′), and no essentialist should reinterpret his essentialist claims in this de dicto fashion, there is no problem with referential opacity.

A similar error is committed by the objection from the fact that objects belong to different classes. It runs as follows: consider, as an example, the claims that

(3) All cyclists are essentially two-legged but not essentially rational and that
(4) All mathematicians are essentially rational but not essentially two-legged,

and consider Joe who is both a mathematician and two-legged. It seems to follow from the above claims that Joe both is and is not

essentially two-legged and essentially rational. So our essentialist claims
have led us to a contradiction, and essentialism should therefore be
rejected. The answer to this objection is once more very simple: both
(3) and (4) are false since cyclists are not essentially two-legged (a
cyclist can lose a leg and still continue to exist, although he cannot
cycle anymore), and mathematicians are not essentially rational (a
mathematician can stop being rational and still continue to exist,
although he cannot then do any more mathematics). The only reason
why one might think that (3) and (4) are true is because one is con-
fusing them with the true claims that

   (3') 'All cyclists are two-legged' is necessarily true while 'all cyclists
       are rational' is not,

and

   (4') 'All mathematicians are rational' is necessarily true while 'all
       mathematicians are two-legged' is not.

So long as one does not reinterpret (3) and (4) so as to mean (3') and
(4'), and no essentialist should interpret essentialist claims in this de
dicto fashion, there is no problem about objects like Joe who belong
to more than one class.

We come then to the much more serious problem of identity through
possible worlds. What has essentialism to do with identity through
possible worlds, and why is there a problem about identity through
possible worlds? To deal with the first question first, the believer in
essentialism seems to believe that objects have properties necessarily,
that there are properties which are not merely had by an object in the
actual world but which would be had by it in all possible worlds (or,
at least, all in which it exists). And this seems equivalent to the idea
that it is had by it in the actual world and by the object identical to
it in any given possible world (or, at least, in any world in which there
is an object identical to it). So, it would appear, essentialist claims are
equivalent to claims involving the concept of identity through possible
worlds and are therefore meaningful only if that notion is meaningful.

As far as the second question is concerned, it is easy to see that the notion of identity through possible worlds cannot be the same as the ordinary notion of identity. Consider, for example, two actual physical objects o_1 and o_2. It is thought to be the case that they are identical just in case they are spatio-temporally continuous (and, perhaps, have certain properties in common).[7] But this cannot be so if o_1 is an actual object and o_2 exists in some possible world. After all, it seems as though an object could be in a possible world in some very different place than it is in the actual world, so we have to allow for the possibility that o_1 is identical with o_2 even though o_1 is in P_1 at t_1 while o_2 is in a very different place P_2 at t_1 and is not therefore spatio-temporally continuous with o_1. The identity of an actual physical object with a possible physical object does not therefore involve any requirement of spatio-temporal continuity, so we must be employing a different conception of identity when we talk about their identity. And similar arguments can be constructed to show that the identity of actual entities that are not physical objects cannot be the same type of identity as the identity of one of those actual entities with a corresponding possible entity. So there is a problem about identity through possible worlds.

It is often thought[8] that the problem of identity through possible worlds is a problem about how we can tell, of some object in a possible world, which, if any, object in the actual world it is identical with, i.e., that the problem of identity through possible worlds is an epistemological problem. That is not the real problem. After all, even if one could not tell in many (or even all) cases, it would not follow, unless one was using some very suspicious verificationist assumption, that there is something wrong with the concept of identity through possible worlds. The real problem is that it is unclear as to what it means for an actual entity e_1 to be identical with an entity e_2 that exists in a possible world, and it is therefore unclear as to what any claim, e.g., an essentialist claim, that involves this concept of identity through possible worlds means.

There are two accounts of identity through possible worlds that should be noted, one due to Chisholm[9] and one due to David Lewis.[10] Chisholm has proposed that, given the assumption that there is, for every object, a set of properties which it has in all possible worlds in which it exists but which is had by no other object in any possible world, one can say that o_2 in a possible world is identical with o_1 in the actual world just in case they both have that set of properties in common. Now there certainly are objects, like numbers and propositions, for which this assumption is plausible. Four is the only object in any world, actual or possible, which is the sum of two and two, and it is the sum of two and two in all worlds in which it exists. The proposition that four is the sum of two and two is the only object in any world, actual or possible, that is the contradictory of the proposition that four is not the sum of two and two, and the former proposition is the contradictory of the latter proposition in all worlds in which it exists. But for objects like chairs and people, there is no particular reason to suppose that the assumption is true and that Chisholm's definition of identity through possible worlds will work. Indeed, the assumption (and therefore Chisholm's definition) seems implausible for such objects. If the set only contains properties that can be had by more than one object in a given world, then one could easily imagine a world in which two different objects, different because they are in different places at the same time, have all of their properties in common. And if the set contains some properties that can be had by only one object in a given world, then it seems unlikely that the object must have that property in all worlds in which it exists. Indeed, it is difficult to think of any such property.

Lewis's proposal is quite different. He would drop all talk about identity through possible worlds and would say rather than an object has a property essentially just in case it has it in the actual world and its counterparts in all possible worlds in which it has one also have that property. The counterpart in a possible world of an object in the actual world resembles the actual object, and nothing else in the possible world resembles it more. Feldman[11] has shown that Lewis's proposal suffers from certain serious defects. But more important, it seems to merely reraise the key problem here. As Lewis himself notes, resemblance in certain respects is obviously going to count more than resemblance in other respects. But what makes one resemblance count more than another? Surely, it is going to be that certain respects are tied up with the object's very nature. But then it is going to be the very same grounds which would determine what are the essential properties of the object. So we get nowhere in trying to understand the essential-accidental distinction by appealing to the idea of a counterpart.

All of these problems disappear if we adopt the theory of essentialism suggested in the first part of this paper. On our theory, it is not necessary that an object have a property in all possible worlds in order that it have it essentially. All that is required is that it have it in the actual world now and in all possible futures in which it exists. Or, to put it another way, a has P essentially just in case a has P and, for all possible future worlds in which there is some o_1 identical with a, o_1 has P. Now the only notion of identity involved in such essentialist claims is that of the identity of some possible future object, some object that exists in the future in a world whose past and present is identical with the past and present of the actual world, with an object that exists now. For such cases, we can just employ the normal criterion of identity governing actual objects of that type.[12] Interestingly enough, Kaplan has noted that[13]

When the worlds have a common part, as when we are considering alternative futures to the present, the individual(s) can be traced back to the common part by the usual continuity conditions and there compared.

He fails to notice, however, that whatever might be required to make sense of all quantified modal claims, nothing more than this limited notion of identity through possible future worlds is required to make sense of essentialist claims.

A.3. The Essential Properties of an Object

What properties does an object have essentially? I want to contrast three possible answers to this question: (1) it has essentially all those properties that it has in all possible worlds; (2) it has essentially all those properties that it actually has and would have in all possible worlds in which it exists; (3) it has essentially all those properties that it actually has and would have in all possible future worlds in which it exists. It seems to me that (1), together with certain additional assumptions, lies behind Kaplan's theory of essentialism and its answer to our question; that (2) lies behind Plantinga's theory of essentialism and its answer to our question; and that (3) lies behind the theory we are presenting here and its answer to our question.

For Kaplan, to say that a has P essentially is to say that there is some name α which necessarily denotes, i.e., denotes in all possible worlds, a and which is such that $\ulcorner P\alpha \urcorner$ is necessarily true. As Kaplan points out, this entails that only abstract objects, which exist necessarily, can have essential properties, for no name can necessarily denote an object that only exists in some possible worlds. Now this result is certainly very strange. Even if one shares Kaplan's lack of intuitions about what properties things like people have essentially, it certainly seems clear that each person, like any other object, is necessarily (and essentially) self-identical. After all, it is not merely an accident that I am self-identical.

What would lead someone to such a strange theory of essentialism? If one believed both (1) and the often-believed[14] claim that non-existent objects have no properties, then one would be led to such a theory. After all, given that assumption about non-existent objects, an object that fails to exist in some world has no properties in that world and cannot therefore, by (1), have any property in any world necessarily or essentially. I suggest therefore that these two beliefs lie behind Kaplan's theory and that what he did was to find some de dicto reinterpretation of modal claims that satisfies the consequence of his assumptions, viz., that only necessarily existing objects have properties essentially. In order, then, to avoid his theory of essentialism, one must drop at least one of his assumptions.

It would be interesting to see what type of theory of essentialism would emerge if one were to drop the assumption that non-existent objects have no properties while retaining (1). It would all depend, of course, upon the view one adopted about the properties had by non-existent objects. If one felt that they only had self-identity as a property, then the resulting theory of essentialism, while richer than Kaplan's theory (since it would allow for concrete objects having some essential properties), would be weaker than Plantinga's theory (which seems to allow for their having more interesting essential properties). But if, more plausibly, you allowed for Pegasus's being a winged horse even in worlds in which he does not exist, then the resulting theory might well be richer than Plantinga's theory. The trouble is that, lacking some good theory, or even some good intuitions, about what properties are had by non-existent objects, it is difficult to see exactly what such a richer theory of essentialism based upon (1) would be like. It is also very unclear as to whether one could find, for such a theory, a de dicto reinterpretation of essentialist claims.

We turn to Plantinga's theory of essentialism which, as he makes clear at the beginning of "World and Essence", is based upon (2). But before looking at its answer as to what properties objects have essentially, we must note one important difficulty with the theory as he presents it. Plantinga supposes that his intuitions about essentialism are captured by the following de dicto reinterpretation of modal claims: an object a has a property P essentially just in case it has P and the proposition expressed by $\ulcorner a$ has non-$P\urcorner$, where $\ulcorner a\urcorner$ is a proper name of a and $\ulcorner P\urcorner$ a proper name of P, or the proposition which would be expressed by $\ulcorner a$ has non-$P\urcorner$, if $\ulcorner a\urcorner$ were a proper name of a and $\ulcorner P\urcorner$ were a proper name of P, is necessarily false. It is difficult to see why he thinks so. After all, he himself says that Socrates has essentially the property of being a non-number, and, given (2), one certainly sees why he thinks so. But is the proposition expressed by $\ulcorner$ Socrates has non-$P\urcorner$,

where 'Socrates' is a proper name of Socrates and $\ulcorner P \urcorner$ is a proper
name of the property of being a non-number, necessarily false? Certainly, that sentence can be used to express a truth providing that
'Socrates' is also the proper name of some number (and we can easily
make it one). And unless one held the view that proper names have
meanings, ones that vary as the reference does, then the proposition
in question would also be true on that occasion. Plantinga, if he is to
stick to (2), must therefore either (a) drop his de dicto reinterpretation
of modal claims, or (b) adopt the implausible view that proper names
have meanings that vary as their reference does, or (c) switch from
propositions (which we can think of for now as ordered pairs of
sentences and meanings) to statements (ordered triplets of sentences,
meanings, and assignments of objects and properties to the non-logical
expressions in the sentence).

Given such an account, based upon (2), what properties do objects
have essentially? Plantinga tells us that Socrates, besides trivially having
with all other objects such essential properties as being colored if red,
has such properties as being identical with Socrates, being a non-number,
and being possibly conscious essentially. He also argues that Socrates
is essentially not a material object. I want to concentrate on the claims
that he is essentially a non-number and essentially possibly conscious.
What support does he offer for these claims and others like them? He
has no arguments and seems to depend solely on his intuitions. But
couldn't I imagine myself, in some possible world, as a number or as
a stone which could not be conscious? Is there anything incoherent
with that supposition?

I do not see how we can possibly answer these questions. The reason
for this is very simple: we lack an account, or even some good intuitions, as to what trans-world identity means in a context in which the
worlds in question are non-overlapping. If we knew what it was for an
object o_1 in one possible world to be identical with an object o_2 in
another possible world, we could see whether o_1's being a person and
o_2's being a stone, or being a number, blocks their being identical.
Lacking such an account, however, we cannot answer these questions

and others like them, and cannot therefore tell whether Plantinga's essentialist claims are correct or not.

To be sure, Plantinga feels that there is no problem about trans-world identity. While I certainly think that he is right in dismissing epistemological versions of that problem, I cannot see how he can dismiss the question of what trans-world identity, through non-overlapping worlds, means. For as we have just seen, in one example that can be generalized, without an answer to that question, we are not in a position to evaluate essentialist claims based upon (2).

We turn finally to our theory which is based upon (3). Here, we do not have to depend upon either a theory or intuitions about things like the properties of non-existent objects or about identity through non-overlapping worlds. Instead, we merely have to depend upon the very familiar and comfortable distinction about the types of changes discussed in the first section of this paper.

What properties are, on this account, essential properties? Well, there are those had by all entities, existence and self-identity. Nothing can continue to exist while losing one of these properties. In addition, you and I are essentially people, that on which the words that I am now reading is written is essentially a piece of paper, etc. And this is just what is wanted, for the essential property that each of these objects has corresponds, as it should, to the sort of thing the object is, to our intuitions about the object's Aristotelian secondary substance.

This last point is extremely important. In most recent discussions of essentialism, the whole emphasis has been on the connection between essential properties and properties that, in some sense or another, the object must have. But there is traditionally this other important connection, the connection between the properties that one has essentially and the kind of thing that one is. Traditionally, the kind of thing that one is is determined by the set of one's essential properties. And it is therefore an advantage of our theory of essentialism that it have as essential the properties that are needed if our kind is to be people, etc.

This leads us to an extremely important question: is it the case, for every property P that is had essentially by some object, that all objects that have it, have it essentially, or are there some properties which are had by some objects essentially and by others accidentally? We shall say that any property had essentially by some object and accidentally by none, whether actual or potential, determines a natural kind, and that the set of objects having that property is a natural kind. Then the question that we have raised really is the question as to whether, on our account, all essential properties (properties had essentially by something) determine natural kinds? It would be very good if the answer to this question were yes, for then the connection between essentialism and this idea of sorts of things would be greatly strengthened.

Unfortunately, our theory of essentialism, like all others, runs prey to the following example of an essential property that is not a natural kind first raised by Plantinga.[15] Let P be some property had essentially by a but not by b, and let Q be some property had accidentally by b. Then the property of being either P or Q is had essentially by a and accidentally by b. So the claim that all essential properties determine natural kinds must be false.

It is important to note that this argument of Plantinga's is perfectly general and applies equally well to any theory of essentialism. Is there any way to meet it? As far as I can see, the only way to do so would be to deny that a has the disjunctive property essentially just because he has one of the properties in question essentially. One way, but certainly not the only way, to do this would be to argue that, although there are such things as disjunctive predicates, there are no such things as disjunctive properties, and, a fortiori, disjunctive properties had essentially. But of course, saying this without some general theory of propertyhood to back it up is merely expressing a pious hope (which is not necessarily to say that it is a bad thing to do).

There is another way in which the connection between essential properties and the sort of thing that one is breaks down. Consider the property of being the person who was in place P_1 at time t_1 and consider Joe who has that property. On our account, Joe has that property essentially, for there is no alteration that he can undergo which would involve his losing it; he loses it, if at all, only when he stops existing. And yet, one would not have supposed intuitively that that property has anything to do with determining the sort of thing that Joe is.

Once more, there is a way to avoid that problem. One can say that while there certainly are such things as tensed predicates and while there certainly are states of affairs which consist in having certain properties at certain times, there are no such things as tensed properties, and, a fortiori, no such things as tensed properties had essentially. But once more, such a claim would need the backing of a theory of propertyhood.

Of course, one might at this point be tempted to conclude that there is no necessary connection between essential properties and natural kinds or, at least, that there is no such connection in the case of at least some essential properties. This would naturally give rise to the question as to which essential properties determine natural kinds and which do not. But I should like to avoid this conclusion; after all, there are other reasons for being unhappy with such things as tensed and disjunctive properties. Still, which move should be made here is a matter for further research.

I conclude, then, that it is possible to construct a straightforward theory of essential properties that is not open to any of the standard objections raised against essentialism and which does allow for some interesting essentialist claims, including, most importantly, those that provide a connection between properties had essentially and the sort of thing that an entity is. But if that connection is to be just as we would like it, we require some theory of propertyhood that enables us to rule out some undesired essential properties on the grounds that they are not properties at all.

Notes

Notes to Chapter One

1. On these and other points, especially the right of the onlooker to kill the pursued even if the pursuer objects to his doing so, see *Talmud, Tractate Sanhedrin,* 72b–75a.

2. This is, essentially, his argument in Section 64 of *Casti Connubii,* reprinted in William J. Gibbons, Ed., *Seven Great Encyclicals* (Glen Rock, N.J.: Paulist Press, 1939), p. 95.

3. This point, and its significance, was first pointed out by R. Huna when he said (*Talmud, Sanhedrin,* 72b) that a pursuer who is a minor can be stopped even by killing him.

4. He would not be the only one responsible. The person who placed the bomb might also be responsible.

5. Punishment is, of course, very different. On this point, see Glanville Williams, *Criminal Law: The General Part* (London: Stevens, 1961), pp. 28–45.

6. This is, presumably, what the Talmud had in mind when it rejects the justification of an abortion on the grounds of pursuit of the mother because "only heaven is pursuing her."

7. Paul Ramsey, "The Morality of Abortion," in J. Rachels, Ed., *Moral Problems* (New York: Harper & Row, 1971), pp. 21–22. It should be noted that Professor Ramsey was discussing craniotomy cases, where both mother and fetus would die otherwise. The significance of that additional factor will be discussed in the next section.

8. The principle of double effect is explained further and applied to questions of war in J. Ford, "The Morality of Obliteration Bombing," and in E. Anscombe, "War and Murder," both in R. Wasserstrom, Ed., *War and Morality* (Belmont, Calif.: Wadsworth Publishing Co., Inc., 1970).

9. For a possible way to draw this distinction, see G. Dworkin and C. Fried, "Intention and Blame" (an unpublished manuscript, hopefully forthcoming).

10. Dworkin and Fried, ibid.

11. One may suppose, however, that that would be a saintly act. But if one is opposed to suicide and unnecessary acts of martyrdom, one may not even suppose this. On this point, see S. Zevin's *Le'or HaHalacha* (Tel Aviv: Zion Publishing, 1957), pp. 14–16.

12. J. Bennett, "Whatever the Consequences," *Analysis,* Vol. 26 (1966), pp. 83–102.

13. (1.) is, essentially, the opinion of R. Yochanan in (*Jerusalem Talmud, Trumah,* Chapter 8) his discussion of the biblical case of Sheva ben Bichri. For a full account of the Talmudic debate on that case, see Maimonides, *Laws of the Foundation of the Tora,* V. 5 and the commentaries on his discussion.

14. This point was made in *Responsa Panim Me'irot* (Sulzbach: 1738), Vol. III, No. 8.

15. *in Libro IV Sententiarum* 1. 1. 3., *ad.* 4.

16. E. Anscombe, "Modern Moral Philosophy," *Philosophy,* Vol. 33 (1958), pp. 1-19.

17. P. Geach, "The Moral Law and the Law of God," in *God and the Soul* (London: Routledge & Kegan Paul, 1969) pp. 117-129.

18. This point helps to shed light upon what is meant by "in a relatively short time." The important thing is that *B* should not suffer any significant losses (in terms of unrealized potential in the period between the time we take his life and the time at which he would have died anyway) because of the taking of his life. Consequently, we must consider the character of his experience in that period as well as its length. It may, for example, be permissible to take *B*'s life even if, had we done nothing, he would have lived for five years, so long as they would have been lived in a coma. It is clear that, as we progressively refine these distinctions, the consensus of intuition is likely to be more and more attenuated. I do not believe that these difficulties are an argument, for example, against the basis of the argument in intuition. One may say at this point that they arise out of the human condition.

It should be noted that, whichever of these conditions we adopt, we are permitting an action that would legally be regarded as murder.

19. P. Foot, "The Problem of Abortion and the Doctrine of Double Effect," in J. Rachels, Ed., *Moral Problems* (New York: Harper & Row, 1971), p. 40.

Notes to Chapter Two

1. J. Thomson, "A Defense of Abortion," *Philosophy and Public Affairs,* Vol. 1 (1971), pp. 47-66.

2. Ibid., p. 53.

3. Ibid., p. 56.

4. Ibid., pp. 55-56. It was, therefore, wrong of me to say, as I did in my article, "Thomson on Abortion," *Philosophy and Public Affairs,* Vol. 1 (1972), pp. 335-340, that "she has not attended to the distinction between our duty to save X's life and our duty not to take it." My argument is rather that she has not sufficiently attended to it, to the point that she could discover that, for example, her whole discussion of Henry Fonda's flying in from the West Coast to save my life is, of course, entirely irrelevant.

5. By a Ms. Andrea Dobrow, of Teaneck, N.J., in the issue of April 26, 1972.

6. Daniel Callahan, *Abortion: Law, Choice, and Morality* (New York: Macmillan, 1970), pp. 453-454.

7. On this point, see *Shulchan Aruch, Yoreh Deah,* Chapter 339; Paul Ramsey, *The Patient as Person* (New Haven: Yale University Press, 1970), Chapter 3; and

my "Voluntary Euthanasia and the Law," forthcoming in M. Kohl, *Beneficent Euthanasia* (Buffalo: Prometheus Press, 1975).

8. This idea of viewing a person as an unappointed agent is based upon the standard interpretation of the Talmudic dictum that "one can act to benefit a person without his appointing you." On this principle, see *Encyclopedia Talmudica* (Jerusalem: Talmudica Press, 1967), pp. 135–198.

9. On the Model Penal Code provisions, see American Law Institute, *Model Penal Code:* Tentative Draft No. 9 (1959).

10. Callahan, *Abortion,* p. 338.

11. Ibid., p. 336.

Notes to Chapter Three

1. It is important to keep in mind that the law exists to prevent the wrong action and not just to enforce the perceptions of whatever portion of society may support it. Cardinal Cushing was right to say that "Catholics do not need the support of the civil law to be faithful to their own religious convictions and they do not need to impose by law their moral views on other members of society." Quoted on p. 165 of Lawrence Lader's *Abortion* (Boston: Beacon Press, 1966). Nevertheless, from Cardinal Cushing's own point of view, the fetus needs the support of the law to prevent its being murdered, and that is quite another issue.

2. "Understanding the Abortion Argument," *Philosophy and Public Affairs,* Vol. 1 (1971), p. 94.

3. Daniel Callahan, *Abortion: Law, Choice, and Morality* (New York: Macmillan, 1970), p. 474.

4. *Population and the American Future* (New York: Commission on Population Growth and the American Future, 1972), p. 173.

5. In G. Harden's famous unpublished lecture delivered in Berkeley in 1964 and distributed by the Society for Human Abortion.

6. Even this principle may need modification to allow for prohibitory laws when the performance leads to undesirable consequences for others although it may not actually interfere with their formal rights. For a further discussion of this issue, see R. Dietze's *In Defense of Property* (Chicago: Henry Regnery Company, 1963), Chapter 4, and the literature cited there.

7. *Amici Curiae Brief of Medical School Deans and Others in Support of Appellant* in the case of *People* v. *Belous,* pp. 25–26.

8. Ibid., pp. 14–18.

9. *People* v. *Belous* (80 *Cal. Rept.* 354), p. 357.

10. *Population and the American Future,* p. 173.

11. Ibid., pp. 173–174.

12. The data from these studies are reported in Callahan, *Abortion,* pp. 201, 226.

13. The data on this issue are reported in Callahan, ibid., Chapter 7.

14. For the various estimates, see Callahan, ibid., pp. 132–135.

15. The foremost proponent of this argument was Robert Drinan, S.J., in his "The Right of the Fetus to be Born," *Dublin Review* (1967–1968).

Notes to Chapter Four

1. On this point, and others in this section, see my *Logic: Theoretical and Applied* (Englewood Cliffs, N.J.: Prentice-Hall, 1973), Section 3.3.

2. John O'Connor, "On Humanity and Abortion," *Natural Law Forum,* Vol. 12 (1968), p. 131.

3. Ibid.

4. Ibid.

5. Ibid.

6. O'Connor's position could be saved if he could legitimately suppose that there are universal moral sensibilities, ones that do not include any prejudicial features. But this supposition seems to be straightforwardly false, so it cannot be used to buttress his theory.

7. Glenville Williams, *The Sanctity of Life and the Criminal Law* (New York: Knopf, 1957), pp. 205–206. Williams seems primarily to intend his argument to deal with the legal issue.

8. John Stuart Mill, in Chapter 5 of *Utilitarianism* (originally published in 1863), tried to meet that objection, but with little success. It has been stressed most recently and most persuasively by John Rawls in his *A Theory of Justice* (Cambridge: Cambridge University Press, 1971).

9. Roger Wertheimer, "Understanding the Abortion Argument," *Philosophy and Public Affairs,* Vol. 1 (1971), pp. 67–95.

10. Ibid., p. 92.

11. Paul Ramsey, "Points in Deciding about Abortion" in *The Morality of Abortion: Legal and Historical Perspectives,* John T. Noonan, Jr., Ed. (Cambridge, Mass.: Harvard University Press, 1970). It should be noted that Ramsey is dubious about the value and importance of these results: "Medical science knows the babies to be present in all essential respects earlier in fetal development than the women who wrote in to *Life* magazine perceived them in the pictures. It is the rational account of the nature of fetal development that matters most."

12. Wertheimer, "Understanding the Abortion Argument," p. 86.

13. Ibid., p. 87.

14. Ibid.

Notes to Chapter Five

1. Paul Ramsey, "Points in Deciding about Abortion," in *The Morality of Abortion: Legal and Historical Perspectives,* John T. Noonan, Jr., Ed. (Cambridge, Mass.: Harvard University Press, 1970), pp. 66–67. In that essay, Ramsey seems to alternate between the moment-of-conception and the time-of-segmentation positions.

2. Noonan, "An Almost Absolute Value in History," in *The Morality of Abortion,* pp. 56–57.

3. Roger Wertheimer, "Understanding the Abortion Argument," *Philosophy and Public Affairs,* Vol. 1 (1971), p. 83.

4. Ramsey, "Points in Deciding about Abortion," p. 66.

5. It is interesting to note that Glanville Williams thinks of the presence of fetal brain activity as a good compromise date for the beginning of fetal humanity, but only because he mistakenly believes that fetal brain activity is first detectable in the seventh month.

6. This argument is sometimes turned around, and rather strangely so. In a letter to the *New York Times* (March 6, 1972), Cyril C. Means, Professor of Constitutional Law at New York Law School, argued as following:

An adult heart donor, suffering from irreversible brain damage, is also a living "human being," but he is no longer a "human person." That is why his life may be ended by the excision of his heart for the benefit of another, the donee, who is still a human person. If there can be "human beings" who are non persons at one end of the life span, why not also at the other end?

Professor Means transfers meaning from what we have called "entity" to what he calls "being" and from our "being" into his "person." This linguistic sleight of hand permits him, at least in his own mind, to evade the point that those who permit the excision of the heart do so precisely because they think that this damage means that the donor has already died and is no longer a human being (in our sense) or a human person (in Means's).

7. Daniel Callahan, *Abortion: Law, Choice, and Morality* (New York: Macmillan, 1970), p. 334.

8. Michael Tooley, "Abortion and Infanticide," *Philosophy and Public Affairs,* Vol. 2 (1972), pp. 37–65.

9. Ibid., p. 44.

10. Ibid., pp. 44–45.

11. Richard B. Brandt, *Ethical Theory* (Englewood Cliffs, N.J.: Prentice-Hall, 1959), p. 438.

12. Ibid., p. 48.

13. John T. Noonan, Jr., "Deciding Who Is Human," *Natural Law Forum,* Vol. 12 (1968), p. 136.

14. A helpful analogue here is the case of a computer. A computer has the potential of operating (even when unplugged) because the structures necessary for operating are present; were they not present, the heap of metal and other materials of the same weight and volume would not have that potential, no matter what the probability of someone's turning it into a computer with the appropriate structures.

15. A whole literature has arisen about this so-called splitting problem. See, for example, Derek Parfit's "Personal Identity," *Philosophical Review,* Vol. 80, (1971), pp. 3–27. But the example of the amoeba shows that the problem must in some way be susceptible to solution.

Notes to Chapter Seven

1. Ludwig Wittgenstein, *Tractatus Logico-Philosophicus* (London: Routledge & Kegan Paul, 1961), 6.4311.

2. I am presupposing—for it would take us too far afield to argue the issue here—that the survival of the soul would not be sufficient for the survival of the human being himself. Indeed, from that perception may arise the insistence of many religions upon the doctrine of resurrection.

3. But perhaps, in light of our discussion in Section 1.2, this feeling is mistaken. I hope to consider this issue on another occasion.

4. David Daube in *Ethics in Medical Progress,* G.W. Wolstenholme and M. O'Connor, Eds. (Boston: Little, Brown and Company, 1966), pp. 190–191.

5. Paul Ramsey, *The Patient as Person* (New Haven: Yale University Press, 1970), p. 103.

6. *Black's Law Dictionary,* 4th ed. (St. Paul, Minn.: West Publishing Co., 1968), p. 106.

7. It is conveniently reprinted in D. R. Cutler's *Updating Life and Death* (Boston: Beacon Press: 1968), pp. 55–63.

8. Interestingly, a jury in Richmond Virginia recently had to deal with a case in which the donor was still breathing, although his brain was destroyed, when his heart was removed. The jury agreed with the doctors that brain death was the determining factor (for a fuller account, see the report in *Newsweek,* June 5, 1972).

9. Cutler, *Updating Life and Death,* pp. 61–62.

10. Ramsey, *The Patient as Person,* p. 96.

11. Saying this raises, of course, a fundamental problem about the rights of animals, especially their right to life. Unless one is prepared to require what might be called advanced abilities from the brain in question—and that would be likely to exclude infants and brain-damaged or severely retarded adults, as well as fetuses, from the class of human beings—the crucial difference between us, who have a strong right to life, and animals, who are commonly regarded as having

a far weaker one, is the species to which they belong. Can that difference in species support the difference in rights, especially when we recognize in animals the very property essential for being human?

On this difficult question, see my "Morality and Religion Reconsidered" in *Philosophy of Religion: The Analytic Approach* (Englewood Cliffs, N.J.: Prentice-Hall, 1974).

12. Daniel Callahan, in *Abortion: Law, Choice, and Morality* (New York: Macmillan, 1970).

13. Ibid., pp. 389–390.

14. Ibid., p. 389.

15. Ibid.

16. We shall adopt the brain-death theory to make our point. A very similar point can obviously be made using Ramsey's theory.

Notes to Chapter Eight
1. That supposition is inevitable unless we adopt the brain-death theory and put very strong requirements on how developed the brain has to be before humanity is present.

Notes to Chapter Nine
1. *Roe* v. *Wade,* 41 *LW* 4229.

2. *Roe,* 41 *LW* 4218.

3. *Roe,* 41 *LW* 4224.

4. *Roe,* 41 *LW* 4226.

5. *Roe,* 41 *LW* 4227.

6. *Roe,* 41 *LW* 4228.

7. *Roe,* 41 *LW* 4228–4229.

8. Ibid.

9. *Roe,* 41 *LW* 4246.

10. This argument is derived from one used (for very different purposes) by William James in *The Will to Believe,* reprinted in William James, *The Will to Believe and Other Essays on Popular Philosophy* (New York: Dover, 1956), pp. 1–31.

11. P. 54 on 41 *LW* 4227, footnote.

Notes to Appendix

1. Baruch Brody, in "Natural Kinds and Real Essences," *Journal of Philosophy,* Vol. 64 (1967), pp. 431–446 and "De Re and De Dicto Interpretations of Modal Logic," *Philosophia,* Vol. 2 (1972), pp. 117–136.

2. Aristotle, *On Generation,* 319b 7–24.

3. In *Physics,* Book I, Chapter 7, and *On Generation,* Book II, Chapter 1.

4. *On Generation,* 319b 2–4.

5. Providing, of course, one has a suitably broad understanding of either what are the properties of abstract objects or of what is a change. If one supposes, however, that changes involve only properties and that not every predicate determines a property, then this remark may need modifying.

6. Those of David Kaplan in "Quantifying In," D. Davidson, and J. Hintikka, *Words and Objections* (Dordrecht: Reidel, 1969) and of Alvin Plantinga in "De Re et De Dicto," *Nous,* Vol. 3 (1969) pp. 235–258 and in "World and Essence," *Philosophical Review,* Vol. 79 (1970), pp. 461–492.

7. I have argued, in "Is There a Philosophical Problem about the Identity of Substances," *Philosophia,* Vol. 1 (1971), pp. 43–59, that there are problems with this standard claim. But even if my alternative theory is adopted, the same point can be made about it.

8. As is suggested by some formulations of the problem in "World and Essence."

9. R. Chisholm, "Identity through Possible Worlds," *Nous,* Vol. 1 (1967), pp. 1–8.

10. David Lewis, "Counterpart Theory and Quantified Moral Logic," *Journal of Philosophy,* Vol. 65 (1968) pp. 113–126.

11. F. Feldman, "Counterparts," *Journal of Philosophy,* Vol. 68 (1971), pp. 406–408.

12. Actually, in order to keep full transitivity of identity, we have to stipulate that future objects are identical just in case they are identical with the same actual object.

13. "Quantifying In," p. 224.

14. Although, I think, false. On this point, see my "Two Recent Contributions to the Theory of Reference," *Studies in the History and Philosophy of Science,* Vol. 2 (1971), pp. 167–175.

15. Plantinga, "World and Essence," p. 465.

Index